READING LACAN

By the same author:

The Daughter's Seduction: Feminism and Psychoanalysis

Intersections: A Reading of Sade with Bataille, Blanchot, and Klossowski

Reading Lacan

JANE GALLOP

Cornell University Press

ITHACA AND LONDON

First published 1985 by Cornell University Press.
Second printing, 1986.
First published, Cornell Paperbacks, 1987.
Second printing, 1988.
International Standard Book Number 0-8014-1585-3 (cloth)
International Standard Book Number 0-8014-9443-5 (paper)
Library of Congress Catalog Card Number 85-7892
Printed in the United States of America
*Librarians: Library of Congress cataloging information
appears on the last page of the book.*

*The paper in this book is acid-free and meets the guidelines for
permanence and durability of the Committee on Production Guidelines
for Book Longevity of the Council on Library Resources.*

FOR DICK

Contents

Contents

Acknowledgments

I thank the John Simon Guggenheim Foundation, Miami University, and the Center for Twentieth Century Studies, University of Wisconsin–Milwaukee, for financial support for this book.

I am grateful to my fall 1979 "Lacan class" at the University of Wisconsin–Milwaukee, who made me feel I had something useful to say about Lacan, and to Bill Regier, who set this book in motion by asking me to write a book on Lacan. Several other people have offered various sorts of crucial support along the way and made it possible for me to finish a book that turned out to be much more difficult to write than I had envisioned. I here acknowledge my gratitude to them: Richard Blau, Herbert Blau, Peter Brooks, James Creech, Shoshana Felman, Bernhard Kendler, Philip Lewis, John Muller, Kay Scheuer, Naomi Schor, Murray Schwartz, and Kathleen Woodward.

I am grateful to Jacques-Alain Miller for permitting me to make my own translations of passages of Lacan's work and to Tavistock Publications and W. W. Norton and Company, Inc., for permission to quote from Lacan's *Ecrits: A Selection*, translated from the French by Alan Sheridan. Copyright © 1977 by Tavistock Publications, Limited.

Acknowledgments

Chapter 3 is a revised version of an article published in *Sub-Stance* 37/38 (1983). Parts of the Prefatory Material and of Chapter 5 were published in different form in *Poetics* 13 (1984).

JANE GALLOP

Milwaukee, Wisconsin

READING LACAN

Prefatory Material

The pedagogical question crucial to Lacan's own teaching will . . . be: *Where does it resist?* Where does a text precisely make no sense, that is *resist interpretation?* Where does what I . . . read resist my understanding? Where is the *ignorance*— the resistance to knowledge—located? And what can I thus *learn* from the locus of that ignorance? How can I interpret *out of* the dynamic ignorance I analytically encounter, both in others and in myself?

—Shoshana Felman, "Psychoanalysis and Education"

PrefaStory

It is generally assumed, in practice if not in theory, that the expression "women's studies" means the study of women, women as the object of study. If unquestioned, however, this assumption creates a problem. In an open letter in *Signs* called "A Problem in Naming," Susan Groag Bell and Mollie Schwartz Rosenhan write: " 'Women's studies' is a misnomer. Moreover the phrase is grammatically incorrect."[1] Yet it would seem that obedience to grammatical rules is not their principal criterion for, in proposing "women studies" as a "viable alternative,"

1. Susan Groag Bell and Mollie Schwartz Rosenhan, "A Problem in Naming: Women Studies—Women's Studies?" *Signs: Journal of Women in Culture and Society* 6, 3 (1981), 540–42.

they write: "Alas, it too is grammatically incorrect since it uses a noun as an adjective."

The problem with "women's studies," as it turns out, may be that it *is* a grammatical construction, which is to say that it is already inscribed within the bounds of language and has a history. According to Bell and Rosenhan, " 'Women's studies' used grammatically means the study of any topic whatever . . . as long as the study itself is performed by women. . . . In its literal meaning, 'women's studies' are subjects studied by women." "Used grammatically" is here synonymous with "in its literal meaning." Perhaps the objection to grammatical impropriety is actually or also an objection to something like nonliteral language, figurative or we might even say ambiguous language, in which a signifier could mean more than one thing, something other than what was intended.

Bell and Rosenhan close their open letter thus: "We know there is much in naming. Let us choose ours with accuracy and purpose." Naming has indeed been recognized as a central feminist concern. Not only is it a case of rejecting our subsumption under a husband's name, but questioning what will be our children's last names, and finally, most radically, questioning our own names, and our mother's names, and so on in generational regress, as always patronyms: identity in our culture being so linked up with patriarchy. And although in theory it has been quite clear that we must reject patriarchal identity as it is manifested in the patronym, in practice the "problem in naming," in terms of our children's and our own names, has remained a big problem, with no clear solution being generally put into practice, however clever some seem in theory.

I would suggest that the discrepancy between the theoretical rejection of patriarchal identity and the practical confusion on the issue of naming is the sign not of some lack of nerve on the part of feminists but of our actually inhabiting a relation to language that makes a tremendous irony of the assertion: "Let us choose our names with accuracy and purpose." I will in this context merely comment that the view of language as a tool—reflected in the words "let us choose," "accuracy," and "purpose"—has been widely called into question, and one of the most brutal of these interrogations—Jacques Lacan's—has linked this language, which inevitably eludes our attempt to use it for our ends, to something Lacan names the Name-of-the-Father.

The problem with "women's studies," what makes Bell and Rosenhan want to lop off its "apostrophe s," is that it is ambiguous. The user cannot keep what they refer to as the "literal" or the "grammatical" meaning, that is, the user cannot keep a certain meaning, embedded in the language but not intended, from returning. The "apostrophe s" is always potentially ambiguous because it can function as either objective or subjective genitive, in other words, studies of women and studies by women.

This formulation of the problem is itself rather suggestive. The word "genitive"—which means "indicative of possession" and which etymologically traces back to *gignere*, to beget—may itself be pregnant with the history of the Name-of-the-Father as the attempt to legislate begetting under a name indicative of possession. The inevitable ambiguity of the genitive (subjective or objective) may resonate not only with the mother as bound up with the infant prior to the latter's ability to distinguish subject and object but also with women's traditional place in culture as neither object nor subject but disturbingly both. Woman's ambiguous cultural place may be precisely the standpoint from which it is possible to muddle the subject/object distinction, that distinction necessary for a certain epistemological relation to the world. Lévi-Strauss says woman is both a sign *and* an exchanger of signs, thus hers is the place in organized culture that evokes another "more primitive" epistemology in which all objects were also considered endowed with subjective status.[2] Might not one of the goals of what we so ambiguously call "women's studies" be to call into question the oppressive effects of an

2. Claude Lévi-Strauss, *The Elementary Structures of Kinship*, trans. James Harle Bell, John Richard von Sturmer, and Rodney Needham (Boston: Beacon Press, 1969), p. 496.

epistemology based on the principle of a clear and nonambiguous distinction of subject and object of knowledge?

Rather than attempt to banish it, I would like to take advantage of the ambiguity of "women's studies," in that it retains woman's traditional peculiar vantage point as neither quite subject nor object, but in a framework which sees that vantage as an advantage and not a shortcoming.

Although Bell and Rosenhan complain of the unintended and vaguer implications of the "study of any topic whatever . . . performed by women," there are those who have affirmed this very connotation, embracing this shamelessly loose definition of our endeavor. The present work assumes that posture: not a prudish correction of the loose and improper but an immodest celebration of the broad.

In her article "Ideological Structure and How Women Are Excluded," Dorothy E. Smith wrote: "We are confronted virtually with the problem of reinventing the world of knowledge, of thought, of symbols and images. Not of course by repudiating everything that has been done but by subjecting it to exacting scrutiny and criticism from the position of women as subject . . . or knower."[3] In "Breaking the Bread," Elaine Marks takes up Smith's position: " 'Women as knower' is the center of our concern. Of all the many exclusions that have, until now, defined women's relation to culture, the most serious are the exclusions that keep us outside the desire for theory and the theory of desire. To be a knower at this point in the history of women's studies means to push thought as far as it will go."[4]

Accepting the "literal," "grammatical" sense of "women's studies," Marks asserts "women as knower" as the "center of our concern." The phrase "women as knower," used by Smith,

3. Dorothy E. Smith, "Ideological Structure and How Women Are Excluded," *Canadian Review of Sociology and Anthropology* 12, 4 (1975), pt. I, p. 367, quoted in Elaine Marks, "Breaking the Bread: Gestures toward Other Structures, Other Discourses," *Bulletin of the Midwest Modern Language Association*, 13 (Spring 1980), 55. Ellipsis Marks's.

4. Marks, "Breaking the Bread," p. 55.

repeated by Marks, is grammatically incorrect: women is plural; knower is singular. This grammatical transgression evokes an entire field of associations. Most immediately, Marks, in this article, characterizes women's studies as "collaborative." More speculatively, certain theorists such as Luce Irigaray have identified the feminine with the plural as opposed to the phallomorphic singular.[5] But finally, might we not say that "women as knower" counteracts the more grammatical and more assimilable "woman as knower"? If the center of women's studies were what any individual woman might know, our new interdiscipline would be just a heteroclite collection. Unless we were to accept an essentialistic definition of women's interests as based in their anatomy, we could not assume that the composite of what all women study would make a coherent whole. That is the absurdity Bell and Rosenhan would guard against. Yet the agrammatical "women as knower" constitutes a new subject of knowledge that is not only female but is also not a single monadic individual. If what a woman knows is different from what a man knows, the feminist understanding of that difference would emphasize not the woman's individual peculiarity but her place in a sexual class, her psychological place in a division of labor. It is the common denominators of the studies done by women—mathematically speaking, it is their intersections and not their unions—which constitute women's studies.

In "Breaking the Bread," Marks not only defines women's studies as studies by women but links this revolution in knowl-

5. See, for example, Luce Irigaray, "Ce sexe qui n'en est pas un" in Irigaray, *Ce sexe qui n'en est pas un* (Paris: Seuil, 1977), pp. 23–32; pp. 23–33 in *This Sex Which Is Not One*, trans. Catherine Porter with Carolyn Burke (Ithaca: Cornell University Press, 1985). Translated as "That Sex which is not One" by Randall Albury and Paul Foss in Paul Foss and Meaghan Morris, eds., *Language, Sexuality, and Subversion* (Darlington, Australia: Feral Publications, 1978), pp. 161–171. Also translated as "This Sex Which Is Not One" by Claudia Reeder in Elaine Marks and Isabelle de Courtivron, eds., *New French Feminisms: An Anthology* (Amherst: University of Massachusetts Press, 1980), pp. 99–106.

edge to what is going on in the *sciences humaines* in France. In seeing a conjunction between the two, Marks is able to imagine a Women's Studies that would no longer be a mere region of knowledge supplementing traditional disciplines, but—by altering not the object but the subject of knowledge, the knower— would call into question what is considered knowledge in any discipline.

Extremely attracted to the notion of women's studies as a force that could revolutionize the very structures of knowledge, I wish to pose the question of what a feminist practice of study might be, beyond the recognizable themes: women and sexual difference. For example, what would be a feminist criticism that neither read women's texts nor read for the representation of women? If women's studies involves an epistemological revolution, how would it effect realms other than those in which women are already the object of knowledge? I have no answers, but rather would like to present the first glimmerings of an idea. In truth, the notion of feminist practice I will entertain was imposed upon me by an unexpected response to my work. My theorizing was stimulated by an event, and the theory remains in the primitive state where it cannot yet abstract itself from the material conditions of its birth.

I was at work on the present book, a book on Lacan. Not a recognizably feminist project, since Lacan is not a woman, nor have I been concerned in this book explicitly to address Lacan's relation to feminism or women, which I have already done in another book.[6] Perhaps naively, I had not considered this a feminist project but had thought of it as a "straight" book on Lacan, a study that addressed the general question of how one could possibly read Lacan's text.

An early, partial version of the manuscript was submitted by the press to a reader, and the reader returned a report that made a great impression on me. It began with the point that the text

6. *The Daughter's Seduction: Feminism and Psychoanalysis* (Ithaca: Cornell University Press, 1982).

was not worthy of publication because it demonstrated inadequate command of the subject matter, adding that I even admitted as much. Returning to this issue at the report's end, the reader suggested that I did not sufficiently grasp the Lacanian theory of sexual identification (again acknowledging that I admitted this) and that I should wait to write about Lacan's theory until I was no longer confused.

The major objection was thus that I was not in command of the material, not in a certain epistemological relation that maintains the proper, unambiguous distance between subject and object of knowledge. More precisely, the main objection was that I was not in command of the material *and* I admitted it. One other objection was tacked on at the very end of the report: that I used the pronoun "she" where the antecedent was not identified as female. The reader found this agrammatical, irritating, and confusing, and considered it an act of aggression on my part.

I am convinced that there is some intrinsic connection between the objection to avowing an inadequate grasp of the material and the objection to the use of a generic "she." The rejection of the automatic generic "he" is, of course, an important topos of feminist writing praxis. But the other gesture was not intended as feminist, but rather simply in the spirit of a Lacanian reading, that is, in keeping with the French revolution in discourse to which Marks refers. Thanks to their joint appearance in my reader's report, I have come to consider that they are, theoretically, the same gesture.

The reader was assuming my reading to be not something other, an alternative approach, but a failure at the only correct sort of reading, one that speaks from a position of mastery over a text. I was and am trying to write in a different relation to the material, from a more unsettling confrontation with its contradictory plurivocity, a sort of encounter I believe is possible only if one relinquishes the usual position of command, and thus writes from a more subjective, vulnerable position. Though I have worked long and hard at Lacan's text and with the various commentaries upon it, rather than present my mastery I am interested in getting at those places where someone who generally knows the text well still finds herself in a position of difficulty. My various mentions of insufficient command of the material are a very central part of my project.

That the reader located my inadequacy particularly in the theory of sexual identification is interesting, since Lacan's theory of sexual identification is precisely a theory of inadequacy, a theory of castration. Lacan's major statement of ethical purpose and therapeutic goal, as far as I am concerned, is that one must assume one's castration. Women have always been considered "castrated" in psychoanalytic thinking. But castration for Lacan is not only sexual; more important, it is also linguistic: we are inevitably bereft of any masterful understanding of language, and can only signify ourselves in a symbolic system that we do not command, that, rather, commands us. For women, Lacan's message that everyone, regardless of his or her organs, is "castrated," represents not a loss but a gain. Only this realization, I believe, can release us from "phallocentrism," one of the effects of which is that one must constantly cover one's inevitable inadequacy in order to have the right to speak. My assumption of my inadequacy and my attempt to read from that position are thus, to my mind, both Lacanian and feminist.

After years of study, I have come to believe Lacan's text impossible to understand fully, impossible to master—and thus a particularly good illustration of everyone's inevitable "castration" in language. The attempt to cover up one's inadequate command of Lacan's text necessitates a violent reduction of the contradictory plurality and ambiguity of that text, just as the assembling of a coherent self necessitates repression. I believe that the pretense of a masterful grasp of Lacan serves only to consolidate the oppressive mystification of the Lacanian institution. Lacan talks insightfully about the analyst as the illusion of the "subject presumed to know." I am trying to undo that illusion rather than shore it up and therefore wish to write from some other position. This project is profoundly feminist. It involves calling into question the phallic illusions of authority.

It is apparent to me now that in my response to the reader's report I was justifying my giving up the position of authority by invoking an authoritative version, an unambiguous sense of Lacan. What does it mean to invoke authority in order to legitimate an attack on authority? This ambiguity, I believe, is what promises the most. To speak without authority is nothing new; the disenfranchised have always so spoken. Simply to refuse authority does not challenge the category distinction between phallic authority and castrated other, between "subject presumed to know" and subject not in command. One can effectively undo authority only from the position of authority, in a way that exposes the illusions of that position *without renouncing it*, so as to permeate the position itself with the connotations of its illusoriness, so as to show that *everyone*, including the "subject presumed to know," is castrated.

Perhaps this ambiguous position—at once assuming and not assuming authority—is finally to be understood through its resemblance to another gesture. I do not simply use the generic "she" in this book, but alternate between "she" and "he," in the hopes of resexualizing the neuter "he," of contaminating it with the sexual difference that seems to reside in the "she." Lacan has said "the phallus can play its role only when veiled."[7] The supposed universality of the pronoun "he" depends on its not connoting the penis, on the veiling of its male sexual attributes. When any possible pronoun for the epistemological subject cannot help but connote sexual difference, then the phallic authority of universal man will have more difficulty pronouncing itself.

7. Jacques Lacan, "La Signification du phallus," in Lacan, *Ecrits* (Paris: Seuil, 1966), p. 692. Translated as "The Signification of the Phallus" by Alan Sheridan in Lacan, *Ecrits: A Selection* (New York: Norton, 1977), p. 288. Also translated as "The Meaning of the Phallus" by Jacqueline Rose in Juliet Mitchell and Jacqueline Rose, eds., *Feminine Sexuality: Jacques Lacan and the école freudienne* (New York: Norton, 1982), p. 82. Throughout this book *Ecrits* will be referred to in text references as *E*, *Ecrits: A Selection* as *S*, and *Feminine Sexuality* as *FS*. (All translations from the French are mine unless otherwise indicated, though I cite existing translations and give page references.)

PrefatHEory

In America, Lacan has been important principally to literary academics. That is now beginning to change. For example, in 1982, I, a literature professor, was invited to the meeting of the American Psychological Association to speak at a session on Lacan and literature. I stated there that I consider it both appropriate and fortuitous that literary critics welcomed Lacan here before psychologists. The famous Freudian slip was Freud's discovery that what interrupts the speaker's intentions has deeper and more shocking truth effects than the intended thought. Lacan says of this that Freud discovered that truth manifests itself in the letter rather than the spirit, that is, in the way things are actually said rather than in the intended meaning. Literary critics learn how to read the letter of the text, how to interpret the style, the form, rather than just reading for content, for ideas. The psychoanalyst learns to listen not so much to her patient's main point as to odd marginal moments, slips of the tongue, unintended disclosures. Freud formulated this psychoanalytic method, but Lacan has generalized it into a way of receiving all discourse, not just the analysand's. There is no better way to read Lacan.

If American psychology is beginning, even in this small way, to receive Lacan—not only to receive but quite relevantly to ask how his work might be applied to literature—then it is urgent to indicate how Lacan might intervene and disrupt our reigning orders of knowledge, our academic disciplinary arrangements. For example, there is a current and much touted crisis in what is called the Humanities. The Humanities are having trouble attracting students and financial support in a societal context where they are severely devalued and subordinated to other, more marketable, modes of knowledge. The Humanities cohabit the traditional center of the academy, what is often called the liberal arts, with the social and natural sciences. The social sciences generally find themselves in between the Humanities and the "hard sciences" and have taken great pains to prove themselves sciences and dissociate themselves from the soft, murky

Humanities. Psychology, which has a shady humanistic past linking it closely with philosophy, has been centrally caught up in this science complex that is *intra*disciplinarily acted out in the distinction between behavioral and clinical psychology. In most institutions the result is an oppressive hierarchy: the behavioralists with their hard data on top of and lacking respect for, or distant and suspicious of, the clinicians. Somehow, this scene reminds me of something. . . .

Lacan's intervention might possibly inaugurate a rearrangement of this disciplinary intercourse—or lack thereof. Psychoanalysis is usually considered to have some association with clinical psychology, that minoritized edge of the social sciences, where science and nonscience do not meet. Yet Lacan, from the beginning of his work, has declared psychoanalysis a science. He has also constantly disdained and decried psychology, made every effort to distinguish psychoanalysis from psychology. He locates the downfall of American psychoanalysis, its betrayal of Freud, in its willing assimilation into a general psychology. Psychology is the construction of the ideological illusion Man, nowadays armed with all the defensive apparati of hard data, as any illusion, the ego foremost, must be defensively armed.

As long as the object of psychoanalytic knowledge is considered to be man (object of the Humanities), psychoanalysis remains a branch of psychology. Through his emphasis on the intersubjective dialogue of the analytic experience as well as his discovery that the ego itself is constituted in an intersubjective relation, Lacan has shifted the object of psychoanalysis. What it as science and practice seeks to discern, is what Lacan, on the first page of *Ecrits,* calls "the man to whom one addresses oneself." But, as we read in his version of Buffon's famous saying on the first page of *Ecrits,* "style is the man to whom one addresses oneself." The object of psychoanalytic study reveals itself as "style."

This has tremendous relevance to the question of the relationship between Lacan and literature, and of the relationship, post-Lacan, between psychoanalysis and literature, the latter perhaps the most effete of the Humanities. Classically a psychoanalytic institute offers a course or two in applied psycho-analysis to its advanced candidates, colonizing literature under the rule of psychoanalytic wisdom. After a few years' experience with psychoanalytic theory and practice, the analytic candidate is considered to have the authority to apply this knowledge to the interpretation of literary texts. In contrast, Lacan asserts that "Freud constantly maintained . . . [literary] training as the prime requisite for the formation of analysts, and . . . he designated the eternal *universitas litterarum* as the ideal place for its institution" (*E*, 494; *S*, 147). Rather than teach psychoanalysis as a basis for understanding literature, Lacan might see psycho-analysis as a regional branch of literary studies.

Psychoanalysis, post-Lacan, is the science not of the psyche (object of the Humanities) but, as Jean-Luc Nancy and Philippe Lacoue-Labarthe put it,[1] of the letter. By allying psychoanalysis first of all to linguistics, that most scientific of the social sciences, but then to philosophy and literature, and yet nonetheless stressing its place as a science, Lacan violates our distinction Humanities/Science. As long as we accept the humanistic notion of the Humanities, they will continue to lose ground, to have a more and more obsolete and subordinate position in the era of the computer. What is called for is a new configuration, a revaluation, not of the Humanities but of something which might be called letters. One node, one context of this shift is the intersection of psychoanalysis and literature.

Psychoanalysis in particular, and clinical psychology more generally, find themselves prejudicially disadvantaged by their suspicious resemblance to the Humanities. Yet, ironically, they unquestioningly accept the ideology which structures that prejudice as they turn around, so to speak, and apply their scientific psychological theories to literature. In her introduction to the *Yale French Studies* issue on psychoanalysis and literature, Shoshana Felman writes: "It is usually felt that psychoanalysis

1. Jean-Luc Nancy and Philippe Lacoue-Labarthe, *Le Titre de la lettre* (Paris: Galilée, 1973). See Chapter 5 below for further discussion of this book.

has much or all to teach us about literature, whereas literature has little or nothing to teach us about psychoanalysis."[2] I have suggested here that, in a reversal of what is "usually felt," we might rather consider psychoanalysis one application of literary studies. Yet this simple reversal will ultimately prove a dead end. By accepting the distinction literature/psychoanalysis, I remain within old disciplinary categories, not up to the rearrangement of the symbolic order promised by a Science of the Letter.

In an attempt to rethink rather than simply reverse the whole issue of "application," we might use a distinction Felman makes between two aspects of psychoanalysis: interpretation and transference. Almost all psychoanalytic approaches to literature to date have been based solely on interpretation. Freudian readings interpret literary texts to show, for example, anal drives or negative oedipal complexes, while Lacanian readings show symbolic fathers and signifying chains. The premier example of this is Lacan's own "Seminar on 'The Purloined Letter,'"[3] which interprets Poe's story to reveal Lacanian intersubjective models at work. The earlier Freudian and the more sophisticated Lacanian readings share an unquestioned application of interpretation to literature. Certain models of the psyche, certain psychological truths discovered in psychoanalysis operate as the revealed latent content of a work of literature.

Traditionally, psychoanalytic interpretations of literature find latent in a literary text meanings which correspond to "the content of the unconscious." Since Lacan denounces psychoanalysts' "fascination" with "the significations revealed in the

2. Shoshana Felman, "To Open the Question," *Yale French Studies* 55–56 (1977), 7.

3. *Ecrits*, pp. 11–41; translated by Jeffrey Mehlman, *Yale French Studies* 48 (1972), 39–72. For a critique of how Lacan uses Poe's fiction simply as illustration of psychoanalytic truth, see Jacques Derrida, "Le Facteur de la vérité" in Derrida, *La Carte postale* (Paris: Flammarion, 1980), pp. 439–524, translated as "The Purveyor of Truth" by Willis Domingo et al., *Yale French Studies* 52 (1975), 31–114. For further discussion of this seminar, see Chapter 2 below.

unconscious" and considers that psychoanalysts have mistakenly attributed the effects of the psychoanalytic "dialectic" to "these significations" because the "dialectic seemed to be immanent in them" (*E*, 513; *S*, 162), any reading that loses the specific dialectic of a text in favor of a fascination with its hidden significations would not be Lacanian. A Lacanian reading thus would not be the uncovering of Lacanian concepts—castration or the Name-of-the-Father—in a literary text.

In his contribution to a volume entitled *Interpreting Lacan*, Stanley A. Leavy, an American psychoanalyst, states that interpretation proceeds along two paths: "the thematic" and "the word, the concrete utterance."[4] Notice that his formulations of the two paths are not parallel: there is no category to match "thematic." Thematic interpretation is easier to formulate; the second path is more awkward. Lacan emphasizes the second path: the insistence on the concrete utterance, the signifier, the letter. Although Leavy voices some concern that thematic interpretation may be reductive, he finally affirms on principle the thematic path, reductive or not: "I do not see how analysis could ever do without [the thematic] entirely; we frequently need to be directed by general guidelines for the interpretation of unconscious content, which does, by any system *justifying the name* of Freudian analysis, *submit* to such formal thematic categories, as the oedipal, the anal, the masochistic, and so forth. Indeed Lacan, although as far as I can tell he does not encourage the interpretation of such categories, has himself introduced new categories" (Leavy, pp. 11–12; emphasis mine).

"Any system justifying the name of Freudian analysis" must be thematic, must reduce the specificity of signifiers to latent, recognizably Freudian or Lacanian themes. Any reading that totally forsakes the thematic path risks losing the bearings of a psychoanalytic identity. Losing the privilege of an institutional legitimation and the prestige of an established body of knowl-

4. Stanley A. Leavy, "The Image and the Word: Further Reflections on Jacques Lacan," in Joseph H. Smith and William Kerrigan, eds. *Interpreting Lacan* (New Haven: Yale University Press, 1983), pp. 11–12.

edge. Interpretation finally must be—Leavy here is right—thematic. That is probably why, despite Lacan's insistence on the letter, on the concrete utterance, Lacanian literary criticism, any system justifying the name of Lacanian analysis, always inevitably uncovers, beneath the play of the signifier, recognizably Lacanian themes.

Julia Kristeva, in her contribution to the same collection, writes that "the propagation of psychoanalysis . . . has shown us, ever since Freud, that interpretation necessarily represents appropriation, and thus an act of desire and murder."[5] This statement about interpretation, read in the context of a book entitled *Interpreting Lacan,* suggests both that we do such out of desire for Lacan and that our act of interpretation constitutes a murder of Lacan. It could serve well as epigraph to the present book. Outside the immediate context, it reminds us that, psychoanalytically, interpretation is always motivated by desire and aggression, by desire to have and to kill, which is to say, interpretation always takes place within a transferential situation.

As long as interpretation is not accompanied by analysis of transference in reading, the authority of psychoanalysis over literature goes unquestioned. Interpretation is always the exercise of power, while transference is the structuring of that authority. To analyze transference is to unmask that structuring, interrupt its efficient operation.

The application of psychoanalysis to literature, like any application of one field to another, is based upon an analogy: in this case, the analogy of psychoanalyst to literary critic. But that analogy operates only in the relation of interpretation. According to Felman, although the literary critic is in the place of the psychoanalyst in the "relation of interpretation," he is in the place of the patient in the "relation of transference." "The text has for us authority—the very type of authority by which Jacques Lacan indeed defines the role of the psychoanalyst in the structure of transference. Like the psychoanalyst viewed by

5. Julia Kristeva, "Within the Microcosm of 'The Talking Cure,'" in Smith and Kerrigan, *Interpreting Lacan,* p. 33.

the patient, the text is viewed by us as 'a subject presumed to know'—as the very place where meaning, and *knowledge* of meaning, reside" (Felman, 7).

At the beginnings of psychoanalysis, Freud believed his practice to be, exclusively, a relation of interpretation.[6] Through the effects of a massive group transference—ideologically appropriate to the reigning orders of knowledge, not only academic but medical—this remains the common notion of the analyst: the analyst is presumed to have a power of insight that allows him to see into the murky depths of the mind, a power to interpret the enigmatic messages of the unconscious. Josef Breuer was the first to discover transference, in the case of Anna O., and it scared him so much he literally ran away. And well he should have, for the discovery of transference is the discovery that the power in analysis is not the analyst's power, but something very powerful that happens between subjects. Freud, able to avoid recognizing the full impact of transference, continued to see it as, on the whole, merely a resented albeit inevitable obstacle to what he considered the major analytic operation, interpretation. This misconception fortunately allowed him to proceed down his fearsome path. Lacan, however, with his formulation of the subject presumed to know and his dialectical conception of analytic practice, has made it necessary to recognize that transference is the whole engine of analysis, that interpretation is hardly more than the medium through which the transference is manifested.

Lacan's general critique of psychoanalysis in the 1950s focused on the nonrecognition of the illusory effects of the transference, which led in ego psychology to the shoring up of the analyst's power. In "The Freudian Thing" he accuses American psychoanalysis of "giv[ing] in to a mirage internal to the func-

6. See, for example Sigmund Freud, "Beyond the Pleasure Principle" in *The Standard Edition of the Complete Psychological Works,* XVIII (London: Hogarth, 1955), 18. All references to Freud's work in this book unless otherwise noted will be to the volumes of the *Standard Edition,* published by Hogarth between 1953 and 1974, henceforth abbreviated *S.E.*

tion itself . . . return[ing] to the reactionary principle that covers over the duality of the one who suffers and the one who heals, with the opposition between the one who knows and the one who does not" (*E, 403; S 115*). Giving in to that mirage, ego psychology theorized that the analyst's "strong" ego would serve as a model for rebuilding the "weak" ego of the patient. Thus the analyst was authorized by his theory to believe in and act out the transferential illusion, becoming the good, strong parent, the ultimate role model, without ever questioning the imaginary structuring of that role, nor how it minoritized the patient and enhanced the analyst's self-deluded prestige.

An attempt to apply Lacan to reading literature must take this critique seriously and thus question the illusions structuring the authority of the psychoanalytic critic. Transference endows the analyst with the magical power to interpret. In the application of psychoanalysis to literature, the literary critic is endowed with the same illusory "power," at least in the relation of interpretation. Anthony Wilden, in his essay on Lacan, mentions that one of the "failings" of "psychoanalytic and psychological approaches to literature" is "the superiority of the symbol hunter, who knows what the author does not know because he has cracked his unconscious code and who confers a privilege on his knowledge."[7] Superiority and privilege here are tied to knowledge. The "symbol hunter" identifies with the position of knowledge, takes on the illusory role of "someone who knows," who knows the unconscious, who knows what the other, the author, does not know. The image of the hunter, however, reminds us that, as Kristeva puts it, interpretation is the act of a murderous desire for appropriation.

Every psychoanalytic critic has a transference onto psychoanalysis, that is, a belief that psychoanalysis is the site of a "knowledge of meaning." I would suggest that, for any critic with such a transference, the most potent antidote is an analysis

7. Anthony Wilden, "Lacan and the Discourse of the Other," in Jacques Lacan, *The Language of the Self: The Function of Language in Psychoanalysis* (Baltimore: Johns Hopkins University Press, 1968), p. 230.

of the effects of transference in reading. Which is not to say that we can simply apply what psychoanalysis has learned about transference to literature. Doing so would merely extend the power hierarchy described above. A Lacanian reading of literature would have to analyze *something like* a "transference" at play between reader and text, but it would have to be careful to attend to the specificity of that something, to the specific dynamic of the relation of reading.

In the relation of transference, the critic is no longer analyst but patient. The position of patient can be terrifying in that it represents, to the critic who in her transference believes in the analyst's mastery, a position of nonmastery. The critic escapes that terror by importing psychoanalytic "wisdom" into the reading dialectic so as to protect herself from what psychoanalysis is really about, the unconscious, as well as from what literature is really about, the letter. The psychoanalytic critic in her refusal to confront literature is like the patient who, in his resistance to his analysis, intelligently discusses psychoanalytic theory on the couch.

Ultimately then, through my reading of Lacan, I seem to be approaching the point of denouncing all psychoanalytic criticism (Lacanian or otherwise) as a resistance to the uncanny effects of literature, as an attempt to suppress the letter under the humanistic guise of the Humanities. Yet that is an abstract point, and if I write here about Lacan and literature, it is because I do not live in that abstract. I am still within the effects of a massive reading transference onto Lacan's texts specifically and psychoanalytic literature more generally. Having denounced the illusory and ideologically oppressive effects of that transference, I nonetheless am in no position simply to give it up. Transference does not, as Freud came to regret, work that way. As a way out from within that transference, I am attempting to do psychoanalytic reading that includes recognition of transference as it is enacted in the process of reading: that is, readings of the symptomatic effects produced by the presumption that the text is the very place "where meaning and *knowledge* of meaning reside."

1

Reading Lacan's Ecrits

In 1966, Jacques Lacan, already a major influence in French thought, published his first book, some nine hundred pages long, a major compilation of his work to that date, entitled *Ecrits*. According to Jean-Michel Palmier, "the publication of the *Ecrits* . . . brought within everyone's reach a voluminous collection of theoretical texts . . . on which each could exercise his perspicacity." Priding myself on perspicacity, some years later, like so many, I reached out and grabbed the volume, available as it was by then in nearly every bookstore in Paris. Clearly within reach, yet, as Palmier warns: "*Ecrits*, this title is a lure."[1]

The title means "writings," promises work written to be read, addressed to the reader, written to be comprehended within the scene of reading, but "it is essentially spoken words that [*Ecrits*] restores to us, fragments of a teaching and of a truth always in waiting or in retreat, always to come or withdrawn, in retirement [*toujours en attente ou en retraite*]" (Palmier, 13). And so the lure: the fish grabs the bait, thinking it can contain and digest it, only to discover the hook, the line that ties the seemingly assimilable to another world, which lures the fish out of its element,

1. Jean-Michel Palmier, *Lacan* (Paris: Editions Universitaires, 1972), pp. 12–13.

beyond the reach of its perspicacity, entices the reader into his own assimilation.

En attente: the truth, the teaching, the signification is not present in the text, but coming soon, promised or hinted. The reader waits, in suspense, suspended from the hook, suspended from the chain of signification. According to François George, "Lacan was able to discern and then make use of the signifier's power of suspense." Lacan's formulation of that "power" appears in *Ecrits:* "The signifier by its nature always anticipates the meaning. . . . As can be seen at the level of the sentence when it is interrupted before the significant term: [e.g.] 'I shall never . . .' The sentence nonetheless makes sense, and all the more oppressively in that the meaning is content to make us wait for it."[2] The signifier has an oppressive power—the power to make us wait. Lacan has understood that power *and,* according to George, takes advantage of it with a style that maximizes the power of suspense.

This oppressiveness is attested to by John Muller and William Richardson, who have written a reader's guide to *Ecrits,* when they describe the experience of reading Lacan as "infuriating" and "extraordinarily painful."[3] Muller and Richardson admit (p. 418): "Summary and critique must wait for another day, when we have greater familiarity . . . with the seminars (many still unpublished), on which most of [the *Ecrits*] are based." Summary and critique, assimilation and digestion, must wait for another day. When all the seminars are published (at this writing, five out of twenty-four have appeared), when all the seminars are understood, then *Ecrits* can be fully and finally read.

2. François George, *L'Effet 'yau de poêle: De Lacan et des lacaniens* (Paris: Hachette, 1979), p. 40. The Lacan quotation is from "L'Instance de la lettre dans l'inconscient ou la raison depuis Freud" in *Ecrits,* p. 502, translated as "The Agency of the Letter in the Unconscious or Reason since Freud" in *Ecrits: A Selection,* p. 152. For further discussion of the Lacan passage, see Chapter 5 below.

3. John P. Muller and William J. Richardson, *Lacan and Language: A Reader's Guide to Ecrits* (New York: International Universities Press, 1982), p. 3 and p. 24.

Or so we would believe, we must believe. If what we have now are but "fragments," when we have the whole we will understand. If we just read more and harder, we will get it. "If we are very studious, we will understand him one day." Thus François Roustang describes a symptom of the transference onto Lacan's theory.[4] "One day," "another day": a teaching and a truth *toujours en attente.*

Ou en retraite: in hiding, withdrawn, in retirement, the signification, the accomplishment of the act of reading is elsewhere, long gone or just left, but missed. According to Stuart Schneiderman, "Lacan's 'saying' . . . can never be accounted for by a written text. It can only be circumscribed."[5] If the *Ecrits* are "essentially spoken words," even if the seminars are all published, they cannot give a sense of that speaking. Lacan's "saying," his teaching, his truth is now *toujours en retraite,* permanently retired. The seminar will not meet again; Lacan is dead.

Schneiderman was fortunate enough to get to Paris before Lacan died, before the seminars ended. He went to ferret Lacan's meaning out of its retreat. "For several years," he recounts (pp. v–vii), "I had labored through his writings. . . . I decided that it would be contradictory for me to continue explicating texts when I knew nothing of the experience from which the texts were drawn. Thus I left Buffalo and a career as a professor of English to become a Lacanian analyst." Lured out of his element, the reader becomes a Lacanian.

A professional reader, after all, he was certainly not lacking in perspicacity. While still in Buffalo, he discerned a lure: "[Lacan's] writings are finely wrought, even overwrought, and they do not easily make sense. In this way they resemble poetry, and like poetry they yield to critical thinking. Yet this resemblance is a ploy, a rhetorical ploy" (p. v). Poetry yields to critical thinking

4. François Roustang, *Un Destin si funeste* (Paris: Minuit, 1976), p. 36. Translated as *Dire Mastery: Discipleship from Freud to Lacan* by Ned Lukacher (Baltimore: Johns Hopkins University Press, 1982), p. 21.

5. Stuart Schneiderman, *Jacques Lacan: The Death of an Intellectual Hero* (Cambridge: Harvard University Press, 1983), p. 181.

("summary and critique," the province of the English professor); poetry does not easily make sense but it is within reach of the professional reader. Lacan's writings appear to be poetry, beckon the literature professor, but are a decoy; they do not yield; they cannot be read. The effort to understand Lacan's text led Schneiderman from Lacan's writings to his "saying," and beyond. His attempt to read Lacan led him to give up a career as a reader and take up the profession of listener.

One option then for the serious reader, a most enticing one, is to follow the text elsewhere. From Buffalo to Paris, from reading to psychoanalysis. Not just *Ecrits* but all writings lead elsewhere. The professional reader, the professor of literature, has learned to recognize and ignore this lure in poetry, in literature. That, in fact, is the first thing we teach our students. The formalization and professionalization of the study of literature have led to the containment of reading within the text, to a sophisticated rejection of the pull of whatever experience the text might allude to, behind or beyond. Yet when it comes to reading theory, psychoanalytic theory for example, the professional reader generally takes quite seriously the reference to extratextual experience. Lacan's writing—"resembling" poetry and yet nonetheless psychoanalytic theory, grounded in a referential practice—may have a particular attraction for the professional reader who, despite her training, cannot quite give up reading as an access to the referent, to experience, cannot quite give up reading to learn about the world.

The title of Lacan's book, the generic "Ecrits," suggests that inside are simply writings, brand unspecified, that the experience of reading *Ecrits* may represent the generic experience of reading writings. Every text, then, might be an indication of an elsewhere, a truth, a teaching, a theory *toujours en attente ou en retraite*. But the compartmentalization that encourages us professionals to treat literature to an attentive, formalistic "reading" while we naively read science or theory referentially has caused us to lose sight of the contradictions and anxieties, has blunted the power of the experience of reading. Reading *Ecrits*, at once ineluctably, infuriatingly, poetry and science, makes the dynamics of the usually domesticated reading experience painfully explicit.

In 1981, after I started working on the present book, I made a trip to Paris with the sole intent of meeting Lacan, of having some sort of personal interview. My unavowed purpose, my unspeakable wish was for him to approve me, tell me I was right, that I had it, for him to author-ize my reading. I was unable to meet him; he was dying. I would never have more than the texts. Dejected, still in Paris, I retreated into my hotel room and into the book I had started as I left Chicago for Paris. I read the last chapter of Edith Wharton's *Age of Innocence*. An American is in Paris, outside the apartment building wherein dwells the woman he has long loved in his mind but not seen for thirty years. He is supposed to go up to see her, but he sits on a bench outside. " 'It's more real to me here than if I went up,' he suddenly heard himself say; and the fear lest that last shadow of reality should lose its edge kept him rooted to his seat." *The Age of Innocence* ends thus: he "got up slowly and walked back alone to his hotel." I thought I understood. He chose not to see her, understanding that in any case he could not really see her whom he had loved for so long. I felt a little better.

A few months later, just after Lacan's death, I entered training analysis with a Freudian analyst in the United States. After two months of analysis I quit. I felt I was searching for the "truth" that glimmered in Lacan's writings, that I was acting out (of) my transference onto Lacan's texts, and that what I wanted—Lacan's knowledge—could not be got by going into analysis. Catherine Clément writes that when she "started an analysis on [her] own account . . . [she] had a strange experience: Lacan's texts . . . became opaque blocks and resisted [her] on all sides."[6] She was getting the experience that was supposedly behind the text, but instead of that clarifying things, the text became opaque: she lost the ability to read. I have tried to go elsewhere

---

6. Catherine Clément, *Vies et légendes de Jacques Lacan* (Paris: Grasset, 1981), p. 217. Translated as *The Lives and Legends of Jacques Lacan* by Arthur Goldhammer (New York: Columbia University Press, 1983), p. 187.

but, whether choice or fate, I will play out my drama in its own scene, the scene of reading.

June 10, 1980: "Lacan gives a last seminar. He announces that it is above all Caracas that occupies him where they work on Lacan without Lacan. 'I am transmitted over there by writing [*par l'écrit*]. It is certain that that's the future. It interests me to know what happens when my person no longer screens what I teach.' "[7]

In 1977 Alan Sheridan translated a number of the *Ecrits*, "bringing them within reach" of the reader of English, non-reader of French, in a volume entitled *Ecrits: A Selection*. Lacan's title was not translated. Already a lure in French, transporting the reader to a scene of oral performance, it becomes, on the cover of the English translation, a more patent indication of an elsewhere, of a text from another language, another culture, another place. Lacan claims he put "Ecrits" on the cover of his collection because *"un écrit* [a writing] in my opinion is made not to be read."[8] In the context of the English translation, the word "écrits" literally cannot be read. And the phrase "a selection" makes explicit what the title of the original hides, that the reader is getting only a "fragment," as Palmier says, of something larger, something elsewhere. The title of the French volume seems to say that Lacan's writings are contained within, not just some of them, on a specific topic or of a specific period. The English title says right up front that the volume you are getting

7. Alice Cherki, "Pour une mémoire" in Jacques Sédat, ed., *Retour à Lacan?* (Paris: Fayard, 1981), p. 72. Cherki is quoting from Lacan's last seminar. She closes her text, written in September 1980, in the wake of Lacan's dissolution of the *école freudienne*, thus: "Undoubtedly . . . to find Lacan again the necessity will make itself felt, in a near future, of returning to the reading of his work as to that of a palimpsest, one of those manuscripts whose first writing has been erased so as to write a new text" (p. 80).

8. Jacques Lacan, *Le Séminaire* XI: *Les quatre concepts fondamentaux de la psychanalyse* (Paris: Seuil, 1973), p. 251. Will henceforth be referred to as S XI.

does not have it all, that the whole of the *Ecrits* is beyond the reach of the reader's perspicacity.

Muller and Richardson: "But if an English translation makes these essays available, it does not thereby make them intelligible. For a normal reader of English, a rebus they remain" (p. 2). If the *Ecrits* are so difficult to read, it is because they are a rebus. In *The Interpretation of Dreams*, Freud says that the dream is a rebus,[9] thus inaugurating the method of Freudian dream-interpretation. A rebus is a sort of picture-puzzle which looks like nonsense but, when separated into elements and interpreted, yields sense; it is a sort of writing that cannot be read and yet which becomes intelligible through painstaking interpretation, through another sort of reading. If we follow Muller and Richardson's clue that the *Ecrits* are a rebus, then the best way to read them would be the Freudian method of separating into elements and associating.

"We call Lacan's writings a rebus . . . because of their style. For the style mimics the subject matter. Lacan not only explicates the unconscious but strives to imitate it" (Muller and Richardson, p. 3). Lacan's style mimics his subject matter. Lacan has understood the working of the unconscious, for example, the dream as a rebus, and he uses his knowledge to forge a style, one that acts out rather than simply describes the unconscious. According to Antoine Vergote, "his discourse on the unconscious wants to come forth like the discourse of the unconscious itself."[10] Likewise, as we have seen, François George holds that "Lacan was able to discern and then make use of the signifier's power of suspense." Lacan writes about the oppressive rule of meaning and in his style he imitates that oppression. He transfers the subject matter of his discourse into his style and makes it present in the actuality of his text. The unconscious or the signifier becomes not only the subject matter but, in the grammatical sense, the subject, the speaker of his discourse.

9. Sigmund Freud, *The Interpretation of Dreams*, S.E. IV, 277–78.

10. Antoine Vergote, "From Freud's 'Other Scene' to Lacan's 'Other,' " in Smith and Kerrigan, eds., *Interpreting Lacan*, p. 217.

Reading Lacan

In an attempt to explain what she calls "the preposterous difficulty of Lacan's style," Juliet Mitchell suggests that "the difficulty of Lacan's style could be said to mirror his theory."[11] The word "mirror" is particularly evocative in the context of Lacan's theory; the Mirror Stage is one of Lacan's best-known formulations. The traditional view of a mirror is that it reflects a self, that it produces a secondary, more or less faithful likeness, an imitation, a translation of an already constituted original self. But Lacan posits that the mirror constructs the self, that the self as organized entity is actually an imitation of the cohesiveness of the mirror image. Mitchell would seem to ground Lacan's difficult style in a preexisting theory: the difficult style reflects a difficult theory. But Lacan's trick with mirrors suggests that the preposterous difficulty, only apparently secondary, actually constructs the theory, constructs the image of the theory, the notion of its coherent identity.

Right after he declares the title *Ecrits* a lure, Palmier asserts: "there is nonetheless one thing that cannot be denied Lacan, we must recognize that he possesses a style." We could deny the value of his theory, deny his contribution to psychoanalysis, deny even that he makes sense, but the one thing we cannot deny is that he possesses a style. Let us explore for a moment the implications of the word "possess" here. One is master of what one possesses; one commands its use; for example, Lacan could use his style to transmit or illustrate his theory, his meaning, his ideas. According to Anthony Wilden, however, "over the years . . . he seems progressively to have become a prisoner of his own style."[12] One reader says Lacan "possesses a style"; another that he is "a prisoner of his own style." The phrase "his own" of course implies possession, but Wilden evokes a more sinister notion of possession, one reminiscent of a certain analysis of bourgeois alienation, in which the property owner is seen

11. Juliet Mitchell, "Introduction—I," in Mitchell and Rose, eds., *Feminine Sexuality*, p. 4.

12. Anthony Wilden, "Translator's Introduction" in Lacan, *Language of the Self*, pp. viii–ix.

as "prisoner of his possessions," working to maintain and keep them.

Clément: "Did he escape from . . . that mastery he said he did not want? . . . Unglue himself from the mastery inherent in teaching. . . . Lacan was losing his balance and falling into a mastery from which he never managed to escape. . . . henceforth the prisoner of a contradictory teaching" (pp. 233–34, trans., pp. 201–2).

After proclaiming Lacan's indubitable style, Palmier quotes from the *Ecrits:* "Every return to Freud that occasions a teaching worthy of the name will be produced by way of the path by which the most hidden truth manifests itself in the revolutions of culture. This path is the only training that we could claim to transmit to those who follow us. It is called: a style" (*E*, 458). This oft-quoted passage closes the text called "Psychoanalysis and Its Teaching," a text that has never been translated into English. The passage clearly says—with a clarity that a reader of Lacan cherishes—that what Lacan is teaching, all that he is teaching, is a style. For Lacan's reader, Lacan's commentator, faced with the undeniable and "preposterous difficulty" of Lacan's style, it is some comfort to be able to quote him saying clearly that the style is what it is all about, the style is the important thing, the message, "the only training we could claim to transmit." I am relieved to know that what I am struggling with is "it," is the main thing. This knowledge helps to justify the struggle. But there is a level at which what the reader is getting can no longer easily be considered Lacan's possession, a reflection of his theory, a transmission of knowledge from teacher to reader.

The phrase "every return . . . that occasions a teaching" in the original French reads "tout retour . . . qui donne matière à un enseignement," literally "every return that gives matter (subject matter, content, substance) to a teaching." When the passage appears in Palmier's book, in place of "matière," matter, we find "manière," manner, in other words, style. The typographical error says it all: the matter of teaching is manner; the subject matter, style.

Following the quotation, Palmier concludes his introduction triumphantly: "Lacan's style attests to an incontestable mastery of the tongue. The associations and plays . . . are never the product of chance, but of a work of rare complexity." Lacan's play with language, that found in the text signed with his name is "never the product of chance," yet the substitution of "manière" for "matière" is presumably what we commonly call an accident and nonetheless, like Lacanian play with the signifier, enhances the meaning through the resources of the signifier. In *The Psychopathology of Everyday Life* Freud sets out to prove that such errors are "never the product of chance." And he does indeed show that they are the product "of a work of rare complexity," but that work—which he elsewhere has occasion to call dream-work or joke-work—is the working of the unconscious. As Lacan has put it, in the lapsus, in the slip, in the typo, someone is speaking, something is speaking, *ça parle*, something is being said. With "manière" for "matière" one can see that something is being said; it is easy to endow the error with signification, to interpret, but we are left with the question: "Who is speaking?"

"The general question is: who is speaking? [*qui parle?*] and it is not without pertinence." Thus says Lacan in *Ecrits,* in "The Freudian Thing."[13] As for an answer, Lacan has a character named Truth say "I speak" and "there is no speech but of/from language," that is, only language speaks. Wilden writes (pp. 184–85): "In any event, the question of who is speaking in the analytic discourse is no different in essence from the problems of locating the speaking subject in any one of the various voices of a literary or philosophical text at any particular moment—the author, the author's second self, the narrator, the questioner, the respondent, the omniscient or the restricted consciousness, the 'I,' the hero, and so forth—although in the case of the literary text the question may be of a more formal than existential importance, and at the same time it may be more difficult." This

13. *Ecrits*, p. 411; *Ecrits: A Selection*, p. 123.

question of who is speaking, a central question for Lacan, is, after all, a very familiar question to the student of literature. When Lacan asks it, in "The Freudian Thing," he makes reference to the subgenre of the detective novel. The question itself occurs in the context of a dramatization with characters such as Truth. If it is Wilden who brings the literarity of Lacan's question to our attention, it may be because, as William Kerrigan tells us, Wilden, the author of the first essay in English devoted to the work of Lacan, was not a psychoanalyst but a graduate student studying Montaigne.[14]

We are accustomed to the question of who is speaking being "more difficult" in literature, but that difficulty is traditionally made tolerable because it is only a "formal" question. It is not "existentially important." Lacan's writing, I would suggest, as well as his theory of the subject in language, renders that question both existentially urgent and literarily difficult at the same time. Literary training prepares us to deal with that difficulty, but it does so by denying any existential importance to the question. Reading Lacan reintricates literary difficulty with existential urgency in the question "Who is speaking?"

In the case of the misplaced "manière," the question of who is speaking remains for the reader generally undecidable. She might of course choose to research it: look up the manuscript and proofs for Palmier's book, determine whether author, typist, copyeditor, or typesetter was responsible. But "responsible" here is an equivocal term because we are likely to conclude that someone's unconscious is responsible. This notion of responsibility along with the notion of "someone's unconscious," an unconscious possessed by someone, keeps us within the realm of mastery of language, whereas this typographical error was probably done against someone's, everyone's will: it is a mistake, one not in any way recognized or taken advantage of by the text. In any case we might conclude that whoever, whatever

14. William Kerrigan, "Introduction," in Smith and Kerrigan, eds., *Interpreting Lacan*, p. xiii.

says "manière," it is not Lacan. As much as this slip enhances Lacan's meaning, it poses some questions relative to Lacan's "incontestable mastery of language."

Clément writes: "If he makes holes in his discourse, it's on purpose; if he splutters, if he stammers, it's not infirmity . . . it's total mastery of the play of words" (p. 44, trans., p. 31). "Total mastery," "incontestable mastery": the absoluteness of these terms is unseemly, a mark of blindness and passion. Palmier wishes to "read Lacan . . . without blindness" and will thus "gladly bracket" Lacan's "fascination" and "charm" (pp. 9–10). Clément admits to having been in love with Lacan's thought, but places that adoration in the past, claims she no longer feels it.[15] Both seem to contradict their position in their declaration of Lacan's absolute mastery.

"Incontestable mastery," "total mastery": a professional reader cannot but suspect the categorical nature of these statements, but I would also like to remember, for example, in the case of Clément, that her claim of Lacan's total mastery must be thought in relation to her assertion that Lacan was trapped in a "mastery he said he did not want," "a mastery from which he never managed to escape" (Clément, 233–34; trans., 201–2). The paradox of Lacan's "mastery" would thus be that he had it against his will, in other words he was not master of his mastery but rather was subjected to it; he was, in every sense, the subject of his own mastery.

It is easy enough for the perspicacious skeptic, ever wary of the possibility of a lure, to proclaim the illusions of those who believe in Lacan. François Roustang castigates those of Lacan's followers who, in their blind transference onto the master of theory, believe that only Lacan can theorize and so become unquestioning "disciples." François George mocks the Lacanians who swallow the gross injustice that no one has the phallus except Lacan: an injustice manifested, for example, in the outrageous fact that, in the Lacanian journal *Scilicet*, all articles were published anonymously except Lacan's, which bore his sig-

15. See my review of Clément's book, *SubStance* 32 (1981), 77–78.

nature. On the whole I subscribe to George's and Roustang's accusations—both are acute analysts of the mechanisms of Lacan's power—but I am also susceptible to the illusions of Lacan's mastery of language. Finally, however, I am more interested in the inevitable intrication of the question of Lacan's mastery with contradiction (Cf. Rose, *FS*, pp. 50n15 and 53n19).

Lacan teaches that language speaks the subject, that the speaker is subjected to language rather than master of it. Lacan's teaching has had its influence. Many intellectuals are convinced that he is right, that he has correctly grasped the workings of language. Thus we see him as having mastered language. But if he has mastered language, then he is not its subject, which would contradict his theory. This is one version of the contradiction. But then if he is forced to contradict his theory of language, he is not in control and that would bear out his theory. The contradiction of Lacan's mastery manifests itself in many different ways. But in any case, it seems, the matter and the manner of Lacan's teachings and writings make mastery no longer possible except as aggravated contradiction.

One way of thinking about such passionately contradictory mastery is via the psychoanalytic concept of transference. Transference always necessarily plays a contradictory role in psychoanalysis. Lacan points out the "contradiction of the function of the transference"[16] in his reading of Freud's paper, "The Dynamics of the Transference." Lacan: "We are constrained to wait for this transference effect so as to be able to interpret, and at the same time, we know that it closes the subject off to our interpretation" (*S* xi, 229; trans., 253). Transference is the major obstacle, the strongest resistance in analysis, and yet nothing happens without transference. It is the necessary precondition for any cure and yet the cure depends upon getting rid of the transference, for the transference is itself a sickness. Both Clément and Roustang see the Lacanians, the "disciples," as main-

16. Lacan, *S* xi, 120. A translation can be found in Jacques Lacan, *The Four Fundamental Concepts of Psychoanalysis*, trans. Alan Sheridan (New York: Norton, 1978), p. 131.

taining an "undissolved"—unresolved and unanalyzed—transference onto Lacan that contradicts the ultimate goal of analysis:
the dissolution of the transference.[17] This transference, in con-
tradicting the values of Lacanian analysis, supports Lacan's
position as master analyst.

The patient endows the analyst with a total mastery of language, like that with which the child endows the parent. From
the patient's point of view, nothing the analyst says is ever the
product of chance, and therefore the patient sets to work interpreting anything the analyst utters, including his spluttering
and stammering. Palmier, who is by no means an unquestioning disciple, writes: "The associations and the plays that embel-
lish it [Lacan's style], even his obscurities, are never the product
of chance." Lacan writes: "Even the psychoanalyst put into
question is credited with a certain infallibility somewhere,
which sometimes will cause the attribution, even to the analyst
put into question, of intentions, concerning a chance gesture" (S
XI, 212; trans., 234).

It is the structure of analysis that produces the transference
effect. Whenever we have this effect, which Lacan names "the
subject presumed to know," we have transference, whether or
not it occurs in an analytic setting. "As soon as there is somewhere a subject presumed to know, there is transference" (S XI,
210; trans., 232). Lacan's writings seem to produce this effect.
But is this due to his style and its ability to mimic psychoanalysis? Or is it due to something in the structure of the reading experience? Or is it perhaps because the reader desires to
"get psychoanalysis," to get that other scene from reading Lacan's text, that she produces the experience Lacan describes as
transference?

In 1973 Lacan wrote that he put "Ecrits" on the cover of his
collection because "un écrit [a writing] in my opinion [à mon sens,

17. See, for example, Clément, Vies et légendes, p. 234; trans., pp. 201–2,
and Roustang, Un Destin, pp. 34–43; trans., pp. 19–26.

literally, in my sense] is made not to be read" (*S* xi, 251). If the *Ecrits* are simply speeches, the best way to read them is to re-store as much as possible of the lost context, the "saying," the experience. But Lacan's sense of writing "not to be read" poses other problems for the reader. The notion that a writing is made not to be read seems an absurdity, a farce. And Lacan's use of the subjective "in my opinion" suggests caprice. More specifi-cally, his use of "in my sense" implies that he can control the sense, decide the sense of the words he uses, that he is not subjected to the signifier's oppression. But he goes on to appeal to a tradition: "this was established well before my discoveries, because after all the written [*l'écrit*] as not-to-be-read, it's Joyce who introduces it."

Lacan situates himself in literary history. Clément also in-scribes Lacan in a literary history, although in an older and more nationalistic tradition: "This obscure clarity rejoins a longstand-ing French tradition: . . . Maurice Scève . . . Mallarmé . . . so many poets" (*Vies et légendes*, 49; trans., 35). If Lacan is impossi-ble to read in the same way that Joyce is impossible, or Mallarmé or Scève, then the professional reader, the student of literature, already knows how to read him.

"The written as not-to-be-read" recalls Roland Barthes's dis-tinction between the readerly (*lisible*) and the writerly (*scriptible*) text. Barthes: "that which can be written today: the writerly. . . . Because the stake of literary work is to make the reader not a consumer but a producer of the text. . . . The writerly text is a perpetual present tense, upon which no consequential word can be posed (which would transform it, fatally, into a past); the writerly text is *us in the process of writing* before the infinite game . . . is . . . stopped . . . by some singular system."[18] Compare what Anthony Wilden says of *Ecrits:* "And when all is said and done, even if the curious mixture of penetration, poet-ry, and wilful obscurity in the *Ecrits* seems designed to force the reader into a perpetual struggle of his own with the text, per-

18. Roland Barthes, *S/Z* (Paris: Seuil, 1970), pp. 10–11.

haps there is a method even in that madness. Lacan has always told his readers that they must 'y mettre du sien' [contribute some of his, her, their own]" (p. 311).

"When all is said and done": all is never said and done; "no consequential word can be posed (which would transform it, fatally, into a past)"; "summary and critique must wait for another day," *toujours en attente*. "When all is said and done": in 1968 at the very end of a book that includes his translation, with extensive commentary, of the longest of the *Ecrits* and an essay knowledgeably situating Lacan in philosophical and linguistic traditions, Wilden acknowledges that "perhaps" it is more than just "madness," "perhaps" there is a "method" to "forc[ing] the reader into a perpetual struggle of his own with the text." In 1970, at the beginning of what has come to serve many students of literature as a method for reading, Barthes valorizes the "perpetual present tense . . . us [the reader] in the process of writing." The reader can no longer be a passive consumer. He must produce; he must contribute something, *y mettre du sien*. The "written not-to-be-read" implicates the reader in its production, drags the reader out of the comfort of her easy chair into a perpetual struggle. But the struggle is not elsewhere; it is perpetually present. What Palmier mistrusts and bemoans as the "fragment" of something "always to come or long gone," Barthes celebrates as perpetually present, always in process, But Barthes is talking about "literary work," whereas Palmier "will view the work of Jacques Lacan through one dimension only: that of his contribution to Freudian theory" (p. 11).

The attitude here will be mixed: I hold both that Lacan writes a writerly text *and* that he contributes to Freudian theory. Hence we enjoy the possibility of an "inconsequential" process of active reading but not without experiencing doubt, even anxiety that we are missing "it," that there is "a teaching and a truth" that are elsewhere, unavailable to our reading, which make sense of the text.

For the American student of literature, reading Lacan, as we have seen, elsewhere is of two sorts: one can give up reading for psychoanalysis and/or one can leave America for Paris. In the second case we might say that the problem of access to some original experience behind the text is a problem of translation. Wilden, who finally if grudgingly recognizes the reader's "perpetual struggle with the text," produces the first lengthy translation of Lacan's writing and refers in his translator's introduction to his "struggle to put this . . . French into . . . English" (p. vii). The recurrence of the word "struggle"—once on the first page of the book, describing the translator's activity, and again on the last page, referring to the reader's situation—might alert us to the resemblance between reading and translation. If the reader must have an active, productive relation to the text, must *y mettre du sien*, then the ideal "writerly" reader is the translator, who literally produces another text, puts his own words there as a reading of the original.

In quoting Barthes I used the terms "readerly" and "writerly," which are from Richard Miller's translation of *S/Z*,[19] because those terms are well known and readily recognizable to the American student of literature. Yet the symmetry of that pair—both elegant neologisms—denies a signifying asymmetry in the French pair: "lisible" and "scriptible." "Lisible" is part of the idiom, a common word meaning "legible, able to be read." "Scriptible," on the other hand, is a learned neologism, one the reader must think (if ever so briefly) to understand, one to which the reader must contribute to get. The words themselves thus enact the distinction between the readerly and the writerly. The specific difficulty in reading "scriptible" gets lost in translation.

Lacan's formulation of the "writing not-to-be-read" appears in a postscript published at the end of the eleventh volume of *Le Séminaire*, but the postscript does not appear in the English translation of that seminar. Lacan goes on to say, in that untranslated postscript, that the sort of writing introduced by Joyce "can hardly be translated at all [*ne se traduit qu'à peine*]." According to Schneiderman (p. 92), Lacan's style "defies trans-

19. Barthes, *S/Z*, trans. Richard Miller (New York: Hill & Wang, 1974), p. 4.

lation and is so thoroughly intricated with the peculiarities of the French language that it cannot be rendered in other languages without serious loss. In his later works he uses many Joycean puns, which are untranslatable." Consonant with Clément's invocation of the tradition of Mallarmé and Scève, it would seem that Lacan's style is peculiarly French, peculiarly intricated with the French language. The English professor would have to go to Paris. Yet who is better versed in the Joycean than professors of English? If this untranslatability is "Joycean," then there is something of the spirit if not the letter of this sort of writing that is quite translatable, quite transportable from country to country, culture to culture, tongue to tongue.

Lacan passes from the notion of the not-to-be-read to the difficulty of translation by means of what is itself a "Joycean pun." "The written as not-to-be-read it's Joyce who introduces it [*l'introduit*], rather I should say: *l'intraduit.*" "Traduit" means "translate"; "intraduit" would produce "intranslate" or "untranslate." "The written as not-to-be-read it's Joyce who untranslates it." Yet this translation loses the pun. To maintain it we could translate "intraduit" as "intraduce": "it's Joyce who introduces it, rather I should say: intraduces it." The correct translation ("untranslate") traduces the whole spirit of the sentence while the traducement carries it rather nicely. Something is lost in translation; something cannot be translated and yet that something is regained in translating, in translation as a process, not a product, in writerly, not readerly translation. The sort of writing not-to-be-read "can hardly be translated at all," *ne se traduit qu'à peine*, literally, can be translated only with pain, misery, sorrow, labor.

Wilden, whose painstaking translation in 1968 of Lacan's "Discours de Rome" ("The Function of Language in Psychoanalysis") was for a decade the major access in English to Lacan, confesses in his translator's introduction (*intraduit?*): "Certainly after the struggle to put this peculiar French into less than peculiar English, the translator may still fear that his unwitting errors will lay him more than usually open to the common charge of being a traitor to his text" (p. vii). Translate, *traduire*, traduce;

traduttore, traditore. Is it faithful to render "peculiar French" into "less than peculiar English"? What is betrayed when we lose the "peculiar"?

"Peculiar" means both "characteristic" and "strange." Lacan's French may be eccentric or his language may be peculiarly French. According to Schneiderman, Lacan's style is "thoroughly intricated with the peculiarities of the French language." Are the *Ecrits* in the tradition of Scève and Mallarmé or in the more recent, translinguistic line of Joyce?

François George finds Lacan's French simply peculiar. His book, a satirical attack on Lacan, begins with a first-person narrative: "not without difficulty [*peine*], I managed to introduce myself into a very closed circle, in the backroom of a café, which, every Friday evening, applied itself to the exegesis of the writings of the great Lacan. . . . I tried to penetrate the secret of the prodigious discourse held there. But, right in the middle of the Latin Quarter, I was like a traveler lost in a faraway land, where they spoke a radically foreign language for which there was neither grammar nor lexicon" (p. 12).

George, a Parisian intellectual, a former student at the Ecole Normale Supérieure, should feel at home in the Latin Quarter, the locus of French student and intellectual life. Yet here he was, feeling not at home but as if lost in a faraway land where the natives spoke Lacanian. The Latin Quarter, of course, owes its name to the historical fact that right in the middle of Paris, in the capital of France, a group of people, students, spoke not French but Latin. Unlike Lacanian, however, Latin is not a "radically foreign language." Students learn Latin through translation; Latin can be translated with a grammar and a dictionary. Lacanian, "with neither grammar nor lexicon," "ne se traduit qu'à peine," can be translated only with difficulty.

In contrast to George, Catherine Clément, who likewise attended the Ecole Normale Supérieure, thinks that Lacan is French "in the very extremity of the language; even in his erudite and old-fashioned way of quoting a text in Latin, in Greek, in any other language . . . and without translation" (pp. 42–43, trans., p. 29). Latin without translation, his text full of unassimilated foreign languages, full of *l'intraduit*, that for Clément is what makes Lacan French, characteristically French. She goes on to say: "And I know intimately that Lacan speaks my language, splendidly. However, infested with foreign erudition it might be, however strewn with exotic vocabulary, it remains French." Just as the Latin Quarter can be found at the heart of the French capital, so foreign erudition and exotic vocabulary inhabit the French language. If the Joycean pun tends to be translinguistic and erudite, then perhaps what Clément lays claim to as French is none other than what we associate with Joyce.

The comparison of Latin and Lacanian brought out by George is suggestive. In a way Latin is a radically foreign language: no one speaks it as a native tongue, its native land being now *toujours en retraite*. Both are always secondary languages, spoken by an educated elite. To carry the comparison pointedly further, Roustang and George, as well as others, have suggested that Lacan's followers form a Church of believers. "The Lacanian school is a machine which snatches the faithful away from mastery [*emprise*] of their mother tongue. . . . It's a question here, in effect, of an essential function of the Church, which must have absolute mastery [*maîtrise*] of language . . . : the mass will thus be said in Lacanian" (George, 111–12).

For George, the speaking subject has mastery, *emprise*, command of his mother tongue. Forced by the Church into an alien language, the subject loses control, cedes it to the alienating institution, which then has absolute mastery, *maîtrise*, a more exploitative power. For Clément, on the other hand, the mother tongue is already thoroughly infested with the alien and the exotic. If I draw heavily here on George's phrase "langue maternelle," mother tongue, it is in order to resonate with the Lacanian recasting of the Oedipal scene as a drama about language. George's melodrama of "snatching away from the mother" suggests an act of violence done to a child happy in his masterful possession of the maternal. This is the view from the Oedipal fantasy: the Father, the Church, the prohibitive agency deprives the child of a happy potent union with the mother. But in fact the mother was already penetrated by the father, by the world. The child actually is unable to command, to possess either mother or language. Even one's native tongue is already an alien chain of signification to which one is subjected as an infant and which one never really masters. The second language—however artificial, however strewn with exotica—does not deprive the speaker of mastery but, because it is explicitly alien, allows her to recognize and assume her status as a linguistic subject, that is, as subjected to the power of the signifier.

Whether oppressive or truth-revealing, there is indeed something about Lacanian discourse that seems to snatch the subject away from a natural, instrumental relation to the mother tongue. And this lure is not just a danger for the native French speaker, but in translation threatens those of us whose mother tongue is English. According to Stanley Leavy, one of the few American psychoanalysts really to attend to Lacan's work, "Lacan comes to us as an exotic, some great uncouth bear speaking a combination of Mallarmean verse and French intellectualese, that turns into an English never before heard on land or sea."[20] Schneiderman, who himself was lured away from homeland and profession, keeps a steady hold on the American idiom but only by remaining alert to a syndrome of Lacanian translation: "the principal danger in translating articles by Lacan or by those who are members of his school is to become so enamored with the 'text' that one renders it in what I would call anglicized French."[21]

The phrase "anglicized French" is troubling. Usually translators stricken with blind fidelity to a French text are accused of committing gallicisms, of gallicizing English, producing "less than peculiar English," or "peculiar English." "Anglicized French" implies that the original, the French text, has been adulterated. That gallicized English might also be called anglicized

---

20. Stanley A. Leavy, "The Image and the Word: Further Reflections on Jacques Lacan," in Smith and Kerrigan, eds., *Interpreting Lacan*, pp. 5–6.

21. Stuart Schneiderman, ed., *Returning to Freud: Clinical Psychoanalysis in the School of Lacan* (New Haven: Yale University Press, 1980), p. viii.

French intraduces us to a middle kingdom where the writing not-to-be-read lures the translator elsewhere, snatches him irretrievably away from the purity of any mother tongue. And he allows himself to be thus ravished because he is "enamored." Such love, love for a text, could perhaps best be called transference, as when the patient falls in love with her analyst. Schneiderman's warning points to a danger of transference: transference impedes translation. Transference: the act or process of transferring, from Latin, *transferre*, to carry across; translation: the act or process of translating, from Latin *translatus*, past participle of *transferre*, to carry across. Translation is the past participle, the already completed transference; transference is the present process in which the original language is not yet behind us. In transference, the would-be translator can fall into *l'intraduit*, an English never before heard on land or sea, wherein the French text is never quite carried across, but falls into a peculiar space between, a tongue no mother could love.

We might say that transference is the "writerly" translation: "a perpetual present tense . . . *us in the process* . . . before the infinite game . . . is . . . stopped" (Barthes, 11). "Writerly" itself is actually but a translation; transference is *scriptible*, and, as we have seen, "scriptible" gets lost in translation, "which would transform it, fatally, into a past." This might allow us to see that Wilden finally moves from "translation" to "transference." On the first page of his introduction he can say "after the struggle to put this . . . French into . . . English," referring to the translator's difficult task which is now past ("after the struggle") as the translator presents the finished product. Yet on the last page of the book, "when all is said and done," where the finished should finish, he encounters the possibility of "a perpetual struggle" where the reader is forced to implicate herself, *y mettre du sien*. Wilden's commentary closes with a glimpse of the resemblance between the experience of the reader (translator) of Lacan and that of the patient in analysis: "even if . . . the *Ecrits* see[m] designed to force the reader into a perpetual struggle of his own with the text, perhaps there is a method even in that madness. Lacan has always told his readers that they must 'y mettre du sien,' and as Hanns Sachs once said: 'An analysis terminates only when the patient realizes it could go on forever' " (p. 311).

As Wilden "terminates" the book (quoted above are the last two sentences of the text), he "realizes it could go on forever." Yet what allows him to end is not simply the realization that the struggle is perpetual, but the reassurance that the reader's unending struggle is *like* the analytic patient's. In other words, the analogy of reader to patient produces a "method" where there otherwise is only "madness." If Lacan's reader is forced to read forever, that might be all right if the very madness indicated that he was understanding, getting it, having an experience which was like psychoanalysis. The reader could likewise be reassured by the fact that at the beginning of his seminar of February 24, 1954, Lacan asserts: "Doing commentary on a text is like doing an analysis."[22]

The present book takes up where Wilden's leaves off, so to speak. What if the reader did not "terminate" when she realized it could go on forever? What if she continued to read, bearing in mind that fact? A reading perhaps not unlike that of Barthes's writerly text. But less lighthearted, less confidently postmodernist, more mindful of the urgency of "getting it," an urgency not unlike that of lessening the neurotic patient's suffering.

This book presupposes the "method" Wilden belatedly acknowledges in the "madness" of the *Ecrits*—that the *Ecrits* seem to put the reader through an experience analogous to analysis: complete with passion, pain, desire to know, transference. Wilden puts it carefully: "the *Ecrits* seem designed to force the reader into a perpetual struggle." Behind the fact of preposterous style there seems to be an intentionality, a mastery planning the reader's experience. To the extent that statements in the text resonate with that experience, the reader can believe it is "designed," believe there is a "method." Otherwise she must face the possibility of her intrication with and attraction to mad-

22. Jacques Lacan, *Le Séminaire* I: *Les écrits techniques de Freud* (Paris: Seuil, 1975), p. 87.

ness. Roustang (p. 52) sympathetically understands that the reason psychoanalysts become disciples to a master (Lacan is his
case in point) is to shield themselves from the threat of madness
in their perpetual struggle.

If Wilden moves from translation to transference, from a past
participle to a perpetual present, the present book begins in
transference. . . . Like a translator, I, a professor of French, see
my task as carrying French writing across to the English-speak-
ing world in which I live. But rather than translate, I would
prefer to transfer, to work in a present process in which the
reader finds himself implicated. I would thus transfer Lacan
from the psychoanalytic scene to the scene of reading.

Not to deny the French psychoanalytic experience, the practice and the theory behind the text, but to recognize that for
many people already, and many more to come, Lacan will be
principally a text, a reading experience, and that this experience
is a real practice, not just a substitute, a specific practice with
peculiar dynamics and feelings that we must try to understand.
The title *Ecrits* is a lure. An *écrit* is made not to be read. Reading
texts is no substitute for the analytic act. Despite all these warn-
ings, but mindful of them all, I have here the project to read
Lacan's *Ecrits*, selectively and in an unmothered tongue.

2

The American other

In 1953 Jacques Lacan is the most influential member of a group that splits off from the Société Psychanalytique de Paris to form the Société Française de Psychanalyse. The latter organization then finds its members are denied affiliation with the International Psychoanalytic Association. Immediately following that split, Lacan is uninvited from presenting a paper at a conference in Rome. However, he goes to Rome anyway and presents his paper, not at the conference but to an audience of his own convocation. Although usually referred to as the "Discours de Rome" or the "Rapport de Rome," this text appears in the *Ecrits* under the title "The Function and Field of Speech and Language in Psychoanalysis." By far the longest of the *Ecrits*, the "Discours" is given lengthy commentary and an extensively annotated translation by Anthony Wilden in *The Language of the Self*. It is the first and most elaborate statement of what we might call classical Lacanian theory, the founding, magisterial statement of the principles of a psychoanalysis that is above all a practice of speech and a theory of the speaking subject. I have chosen not to do a reading of this central text for the present book; the only reason I can give is that the sheer length of the "Discours" intimidates me.

In her biography of Lacan, Catherine Clément says of the

"Discours," "Lacan had just met his myth."[1] It is here that Lacan begins to talk like Lacan—at least like a certain Lacan, the one we are reading in the present book. With the important exception of "The Mirror Stage" (Chap. 3 below), this book presents readings of Lacan texts from one period, the period that begins with the split of 1953 and the "Discours de Rome." In 1964 another event marks its close: the Société Française de Psychanalyse is admitted to the International Psychoanalytic Association on the condition that Lacan be excluded from its teaching, training analyses, and supervision.[2] Many members choose international recognition over solidarity with Lacan. He and those who stay with him do not again seek entry into the international association. On June 21, 1964, Lacan founds the Ecole Freudienne de Paris with the words "I found, as alone as I have always been in my relation to the psychoanalytic cause, the French school of psychoanalysis."[3] In 1980 he unilaterally dissolves this same school, underlining his solitude. Lacan says he has always been alone. His statement of 1964 retroactively recasts his past as a path leading to his inevitable solitude. But before that, he has not yet taken on, fully assumed, that solitary destiny. In Clément's terms, although in 1953 he met his myth, he did not recognize it as his until eleven years later.

From 1964 on, Lacan is alone in that he is speaking only to other Lacanians. There are more battles, but they are all between those who are on the same side relative to the 1953 split, between those who admit the basic precept of the "Discours de Rome." In the period with which the present book is concerned, Lacan is still involved—albeit in an angry, adversarial way—with the international psychoanalytic community, especially with the American ego psychologists who predominate there.

1. Clément, *Vies et légendes de Jacques Lacan*, p. 131; trans., p. 112.

2. Jacques-Alain Miller has edited a volume of documentation for each of these events: *La Scission de 1953: La communauté psychanalytique en France* I (Paris: Bibliothèque d'*Ornicar?*, 1976), and *L'Excommunication: La communauté psychanalytique en France* II (Paris: Bibliothèque d'*Ornicar?*, 1977).

3. "Fondation de l'EFP par Jacques Lacan," in Miller, ed., *L'Excommunication*, p. 149.

After 1964 he is talking only within a French context, having once and for all accepted his exclusion from official international psychoanalytic society. But in the period I am examining he is still concerned with American psychoanalysis, still talking to America, albeit in anger and disdain. It is perhaps for this reason that the texts of this period speak to an American public.

In these writings, that is, in those that make up the bulk of the *Ecrits*, Lacan attacks America. Lacan's "adversary" in the *Ecrits* is generally understood to be ego psychology, that offshoot of psychoanalysis whose home ground is the United States. Lacan considers ego psychology a betrayal of psychoanalysis, a repression of the unconscious, and a self-righteous manipulation of patients. But he does not limit his attacks to American psychoanalysis. There is a more general campaign against the "American way of life." Ego psychology is seen to be a deformation of psychoanalysis peculiarly suited to American values, giving the American people what they want. In fact, although the founders of ego psychology—Heinz Hartmann, Ernst Kris, and Rudolf Loewenstein—are all immigrants to the United States, Lacan emphasizes the association between the evil and America.

In the index of concepts at the back of *Ecrits*, the last category is "L'idéologie de la libre-entreprise" (the ideology of free enterprise). This category is explained and amplified by the following list: "American way of life, human relations, human engeneering [*sic*], braintrust, success, happiness, happy end, basic personality, pattern, etc."[4] Unlike the rest of the index in the original French text, the elements in this list are all in English. A glance at any of the pages represented by the numbers that follow quickly ascertains that these terms are all objects of derision, sarcasm, or outright attack. The problem of translating or transferring the *Ecrits* into the American scene is not simply to get the *Ecrits* into America, but what to do about the America that is already in the *Ecrits*. That internal America remains so alien that Lacan continually refers to it in English (in American

---

4. *Ecrits*, p. 902; *Ecrits: A Selection*, p. 331. The index is compiled by Jacques-Alain Miller.

words). His refusal to accept America, to have any exchange with it, to assimilate it, is marked by his refusal to translate the words.

Lacan will not assimilate America. And vice versa. The most common reaction to Lacan here has been rejection. This may actually be fortunate. The American ease of assimilation, the American power of cooptation, can serve to cover over America's ideology, investments, and identity. If Lacan can provoke a resistance, then it may be that Lacan offers America the possibility of understanding itself better.

Not just fortunate for America, but also for Lacan. Lacan has many followers in France and elsewhere in Europe. Such a following is not an unmixed blessing. The refusal to translate, although an act of rejection, also has the effect of keeping the signifier (the material specificity of the sign) and not trying to reduce it to signified (a meaning) that another signifier could represent just as well. For Lacan, the truth is to be found in the signifier—in the letter, not the spirit. The refusal to translate, Lacan's and America's refusal to translate each other, may have the happy result that the evidence of the truth, the materiality of the signifier, has not yet been covered over. It is still there to be read.

America has not been so unwilling to assimilate Freud. In "La Chose freudienne," Lacan recalls that as Freud and Jung arrived in the port of New York in view of the Statue of Liberty, Freud said, "They don't realize we're bringing them the plague." Lacan says that this remark "is sent back to [Freud] as a penalty for hubris" (E, 403; S, 116). The Statue of Liberty provides an illuminating background for the remark; its inscription "Give me your tired, your poor . . . ," announces America's project to assimilate everything, including that rejected by the rest of the world. It is worth noting that the statue is a gift from France, that there is a smaller replica of it in Paris, that this image of America as Melting Pot may in some way already be coming from Paris.

Freud's hubris, his pride, prevented him from recognizing the power of America, of his supposed "victim." The penalty for this hubris is that the remark "is sent back to him [lui est ren-

voyé]," like an unopened letter. Return to sender. If, as Lacan emphasized in "La Chose freudienne," Freud's truth is in the letter, this one is not read. As Lacan goes on to say, "Nemesis has only to take him at his word." Freud's hubris receives its just punishment. As he predicted, America does not realize, does not *ever* realize he has brought the plague. Our best defense against this "plague" is our lack of recognition, lack of resistance. We assimilate Freud, make psychoanalysis American.

In our attempt to read Lacan here, we must cope not only with the America that is in Lacan's France (the replica of the Statue of Liberty) but also with the France that is already in America. Lacan's marginal acceptance in this country has been, on the whole, strongest in academic French departments whose approval of him may represent identification with his anti-American stance. The American words (success, happiness, etc.) that constitute an unassimilated, internal colony in Lacan's French text may find their mirror image in the status of American French departments that speak and think in French, that refuse to translate French into America.

Yet if one's project is to carry Lacan across, it cannot be accomplished within the confines of a francophile colony internal to America; having arrived here, he would still be there. If my ultimate project is to foster some sort of dialogue between Lacan and America, then the dialogue cannot be a play of mirrors. A mirror image can be understood as either a specular opposite (right vs. left) or as something identical. Lacan in fact situates opposites, rivalry, and aggressivity in identification; the adversary is simply one version of the alter ego. He terms the type of relation between the self and its mirror image (either as adversary or as identity) "imaginary." "The imaginary" (a noun for Lacan) is the realm where intersubjective structures are covered over by mirroring. Lacan's writings contain an implicit ethical imperative to break the mirror, an imperative to disrupt the imaginary in order to reach "the symbolic." One might say that "the symbolic"—which for Lacan is the register of language, social exchange, and radical intersubjectivity—would be the locus of dialogue. My project to provoke a dialogue between these two adversaries might be understood as an attempt to break out of an imaginary reading of Lacan and reach the symbolic.

But the imaginary and the symbolic themselves tend to become adversarial terms in a systematic reading of Lacan. Inasmuch as anyone would be "for" the symbolic and "against" the imaginary, he would be operating in the imaginary. Ironically, the ethical imperative to accede to the symbolic and vigilantly to resist the imaginary is itself mired in the imaginary.[5] Which is not to dismiss the value of the ethic. To give a reading of Lacan that is faithful to this ethic means that the reading must not always side "with" Lacan, that it must be suspicious of the imaginary (egotistical or adversarial) dimension of his work.

The difference between an imaginary reading and a symbolic reading is subtle indeed. Before I can attempt to set forth the possibilities for a symbolic reading of *Ecrits* in America, I would like to examine the relationship between the imaginary and the symbolic, the double and the mirror, as they operate in Lacan.

If the difference between the imaginary and the symbolic is understood as an opposition between two identities, we can be sure we have given an imaginary reading of the terms. It could be said that the symbolic can be encountered only as a tear in the fabric of the imaginary, a revealing interruption. The paths to the symbolic are thus *in* the imaginary. The symbolic can be reached only by not trying to avoid the imaginary, by knowingly being *in* the imaginary. Likewise, mastery of the illusions that psychoanalysis calls transference can be attained only by falling prey to those illusions, by losing one's position of objectivity, control, or mastery in relation to them.

The imaginary is made up of *imagoes*. An imago is an uncon-

5. Fredric Jameson makes a similar point, in a different context. Jameson, "Imaginary and Symbolic in Lacan: Marxism, Psychoanalytic Criticism, and the Problem of the Subject," *Yale French Studies* 55–56 (1977), 350 and 378.

scious image or cliché "which preferentially orients the way in which the subject apprehends other people."[6] In the imaginary mode, one's understanding of other people is shaped by one's own imagoes. The perceived other is actually, at least in part, a projection. Psychoanalysis is an attempt to recognize the subject's imagoes in order to ascertain their deforming effect upon the subject's understanding of her relationships. The point is not to give up the imagoes (an impossible task) nor to create better ones (any static image will deform the perception of the dynamics of intersubjectivity). But, in the symbolic register, the subject understands these imagoes as structuring projections.

Lacan condemns ego psychology as hopelessly mired in the imaginary because it promotes an identification between the analysand's ego and the analyst's. The ego, for Lacan, is an imago. The enterprise of ego psychology reshapes the analysand's imagoes into ones that better correspond to "reality,"— that is, to the analyst's reality, which can only mean to the analyst's imagoes. The analysand has no way of grasping the working of his imagoes. He has simply substituted the analyst's imaginary for his own. But this imaginary is now certified by the analyst as "real." The successful mirroring that goes on in ego psychology constitutes a failure to reach the symbolic.

Yet the difference between a "good" analysis and an "imaginary" one is extremely subtle. A "good" analysis does not avoid the imaginary or condemn the mirror. On the contrary.

In "Aggressivity in Psychoanalysis," Lacan insists that the "imago is revealed only in so far as our attitude offers the subject the pure mirror of an unruffled surface" (E, 109; S, 15). The analyst should be a mirror for the analysand. A mirror but not a mirror image. "Unruffled surface" translates "surface sans accidents." "Accidents" in French means, according to Le Petit Ror-

6. Psychoanalytic definitions from Jean Laplanche and Jean-Baptiste Pontalis, *Vocabulaire de la psychanalyse* (Paris: PUF, 1967). This reference from p. 196. The *Vocabulaire* has been translated by Donald Nicholson-Smith as *The Language of Psychoanalysis* (London: Hogarth, 1973).

bert, "that which breaks uniformity," in a terrain, for example. But it also means, philosophically, "that which 'is added' to the essence, can be modified or suppressed without altering its nature. An accessory, secondary fact." To be a "surface sans accidents" is to be a surface without attributes, without any characteristic except the pure fact of surface. This is the analyst's neutrality. In so far as she is an unruffled surface, she can serve as a screen for the analysand's personality or values or knowledge. It is not the analyst's ego but her neutrality that should mirror the analysand. Psychoanalysis should not be an encounter with a likeness or a double, but with a mirror.

Yet, how does one distinguish a mirror from a mirror image? The mirror itself, devoid of any content, cannot be perceived, but is simply that which structures the image, makes it possible. In the ethical imperative to be in the symbolic, the charge is to look into the mirror and see not the image but the mirror itself.

Beginning a new paragraph, Lacan goes on to say, "But imagine what would take place in a patient who saw in his analyst an exact replica of himself." In this case the analyst is not mirror but likeness. "Everyone feels," Lacan continues, "that the excess of aggressive tension would set up such an obstacle to the manifestation of transference that its useful effect could be produced only with extreme sluggishness." For Lacan, aggression is produced in response to the mirror image. There is a rivalry over which is the self and which the other, which the ego and which the replica. This relation of ego and alter ego would block the *manifestation* of the transference, that is, it would obstruct the revelation of the imagoes. Transference would be going on but could not be recognized as such because what is projected would appear to be actually "out there." The imaginary would seem real. It is the imaginary as imaginary which constitutes the symbolic.[7] In this case the analyst would approximate to what

7. I presented this chapter to a seminar taught by John Muller and William Richardson at the University of Massachusetts, three years after the chapter was drafted. Richardson asked about this sentence—"It is the imaginary as imaginary which constitutes the symbolic." He was not convinced. Although three years earlier I had been convinced that this was a

he is "presumed" to be, and thus the action of presumption or projection would pass unnoticed.

Lacan continues: "If we will imagine it, as an extreme case, lived in the mode of strangeness proper to apprehensions of the *double*, this situation would set off an uncontrollable anxiety." Sheridan translates the end of this sentence as "an uncontrollable anxiety on the part of the analysand." "On the part of the analysand" is his addition (projection?). Nothing in Lacan's text identifies whose anxiety it is. Sheridan's specification has the effect of controlling the anxiety. The anxiety produced by the "double" is precisely the question of whose anxiety it is. Sheridan would avoid the mirroring of the double, would never fall for the illusion of identity between analyst and analysand. But at the price of maintaining another illusion. In believing the analyst immune from anxiety, in believing the analyst "in control," he is presuming the analyst "to know."

Lacan uses the word "imagine" twice in this paragraph: "But imagine what would take place in a patient who saw in his analyst an exact replica of himself. If we will imagine it, as an extreme case, . . . this situation would set off an uncontrollable anxiety." These "imagines" recall the imago of the preceding sentence. "Our" imagining would appear to be merely the rhetorical frame for the content of what Lacan is talking about. We are imagining what might happen within the analytic situation. But the repetition of the word "imagine" creates an insistence that recalls "imago," that calls attention to an echo between the frame and the image, between our imagining and what we are imagining. How can we tell the frame from the image? How can we tell the mirror from the likeness?

"If we will imagine it, . . . this situation would set off an uncontrollable anxiety." "Our" imagining might itself lead to

---

new and illuminating understanding of the relationship of the imaginary and the symbolic, I no longer had the conviction, only the memory of the conviction. A day later Muller pointed out to me that, in his epilogue to *Interpreting Lacan*, Joseph H. Smith says something quite similar: "It is in the light of the Symbolic order that the Imaginary is situated *as* Imaginary" (p. 268).

the anxiety. If the analysand could be sure that the analyst was not anxious, or was at least in control of the anxiety, then the analysand would not experience the analyst as a double, would be able to distinguish between the anxious one and the not-anxious one. What is "uncontrollable" about the anxiety is that it "belongs" to no one, is in no one's possession.

Sheridan's presumption that the anxiety must be the analysand's finds an interesting echo in a scathing critique of Lacan, made by Jacques Derrida, who accuses him of avoiding and repressing manifestations of the double. "By neutralizing the double," writes Derrida, "[Lacan] does everything necessary to avoid what *Aggressivity in Psychoanalysis* calls 'uncontrollable anxiety.' That of the analysand, of course."[8]

Although when Derrida writes "that of the analysand," he is not quoting Lacan, he seems to believe he is bringing out an implicit assumption of Lacan's text. His "of course" marks that he is being ironic. Derrida presumes not that the analyst/Lacan is immune from anxiety, but that Lacan presumes that the analyst/Lacan is immune from anxiety. Nonetheless, the difference between Derrida's ironic comment on the analyst's self-delusion of mastery and Sheridan's apparently more naive illusion of the analyst's mastery is not so very great. It may merely be the difference between a negative and a positive transference. After all, they both project the same thought into Lacan's text, a thought which "preferentially orients apprehension" of the text. As I have tried to show, the Lacan paragraph in question, with its "imagines," can provoke a kind of anxious uncertainty about whose anxieties and whose imagoes are in question. Derrida says that Lacan is avoiding the double. But one could like-

8. Jacques Derrida, "Le Facteur de la vérité" in *La Carte postale* (Paris: Aubier-Flammarion, 1980), p. 489. "Le Facteur" was originaly published in *Poétique* 21 (1975). Although most of Derrida's text is translated into American—"The Purveyor of Truth," *Yale French Studies* 52 (1975)—this quotation is from a portion that has unfortunately been omitted from the translation. For a brilliant reading of the Derrida-Lacan confrontation around Poe, see Barbara Johnson, "The Frame of Reference," *Yale French Studies* 55–56 (1977).

wise say that Derrida and Sheridan are avoiding some anxiety-producing double by attributing a certainty and a distinction between analyst and analysand that is not there in Lacan's paragraph, which is precisely about a confusion between analyst and analysand.

Lacan's paragraph begins "mais qu'on imagine," which I have translated "but imagine." Literally, however, in the French, the imagining is being done neither by interlocutor nor speaker, neither by analyst or analysand, but by the impersonal pronoun "on." The imagining is done by a subject with no particular attributes. The impersonality of "on" recalls the analyst's neutrality, while the verb "imagine" recalls the analysand projecting imagoes. Thus both subject and verb are elements of the sentence immediately preceding ("the imago is revealed only in so far as our attitude offers the subject the pure mirror of an unruffled surface"). "On imagine" condenses these two terms, condensing the projector and the screen. It may be that the success of Lacan's paragraph is that, in its neutral refusal to decide to whom Lacan attributes the anxiety, it serves as a surface for the *reader's* projections. The text would thus produce manifestations of transference.

Now I am presuming Lacan "knows," presuming that he is controlling the transference, manipulating it, that he is master of its illusions. But even if I were wrong, I would, in some way, be right. Which is to say that even if he were not in control, even if he had no idea of this potential effect of his words, the effect of those words would have nonetheless made me project his knowledge and thus indeed provoked a transference, and at the very moment he is speaking of transference. Whether he knows or not, the very undecidability of the question of whether or not he knows corresponds to the analytic technique of neutrality. Analytic neutrality cannot be actual impartiality. The analyst is a subject and thus cannot avoid having values, prejudices, and opinions. Analytic neutrality is rather a technique that prevents the analysand from determining what those opinions are. Therefore whatever opinion the analysand attributes to the analyst is likely to betray the analysand's imagoes.

The coincidence of Sheridan's and Derrida's interpretations of Lacan is quite apt for a return to the problem of an American "translation" of Lacan.

Sheridan's translation is available for the American who does not read French. Yet from this example, it is clear that the translation is prey to distortion, is unwittingly, unreflectedly, deformed by the translator's imaginary. Perhaps the problem is that any translator, any person who devotes great time and effort to conveying someone else's words, is already operating with a strong identification, already wishing to operate as a double. A translation that presents itself as a faithful rendering of the original operates like the imaginary, which presents itself as an apprehension of the real. If the symbolic is a glimpse of the imaginary *as* imaginary, then a "translation" of a translation may offer some grasp on the translation, some possibility of going beyond the translation's "imaginary."

The relationship between Derrida and an American "translation" of Lacan is less direct, but perhaps ultimately more illuminating. Derrida is neither translating Lacan, nor writing in English or directly for an American audience. But a certain Franco-American exchange is already operating as a background for the confrontation between Derrida and Lacan. Derrida's critique is a reading of Lacan's reading of Edgar Allan Poe's story "The Purloined Letter." Derrida not only accuses Lacan of avoiding doubles in that story, but also of ignoring the persona Lacan calls the "general narrator." These two avoidances may actually be one, since, as Derrida shows,[9] the general narrator and the hero, Dupin, are doubles of each other. But what is perhaps most interesting, in our context, is that this is a relation of identification between a Frenchman and an American.

Thus, with the help of Derrida's reading, we see that Lacan is ignoring some Franco-American imaginary operating in the Poe story between Dupin and the narrator. But there is another Franco-American relation that Lacan does bring out in his text. In the "Seminar on 'The Purloined Letter'" Lacan introduces

9. See, for example, Derrida, *La Carte postale*, p. 518; trans., pp. 107–8.

his subject as "the tale which Baudelaire translated under the title *La Lettre volée.*"[10] Lacan explicitly introduces his subject as a translation. Baudelaire is mentioned a full page before Poe. In the American translation of Lacan's text, this oddness is further emphasized since "la lettre volée" are the first French words that the reader encounters in the text. In a translation, words left in the original language usually represent something so particular to the original context that they cannot be assimilated into the new language. But in this case what resists the "melting pot" of the American text is the French title for an American story. What cannot be translated into American is some America that is already in French.

The appearance of these French words in the American text is mirrored by an appearance of the American title untranslated in the French text. Lacan writes, "it remains, nevertheless, that Baudelaire, despite his devotion, betrayed Poe by translating as 'la lettre volée' his title: *the purloined letter*" (*E,* 29; trans., 59). Lacan then goes on to discuss the Anglo-French etymology of the word "purloined." If Lacan begins by introducing the story as Baudelaire's translation only to later accuse Baudelaire of traducement in his *traduction,* we are perhaps brought to the realization that we must inevitably deal with "bad translations." In other words, the imaginary will always block us from apprehending the real (the original text). But at least we can try to catch the functioning distortions of translation as translation (not the real, but the symbolic).

The "Seminar on 'The Purloined Letter'" is the opening essay of *Ecrits.* When a short collection of *Ecrits* is later published in pocketbook format, it is explicitly retained as the opening essay.[11] Thus a potential translator of *Ecrits* into English immediately meets his mirror image in Baudelaire, translator/betrayer of Poe. This encounter entails a danger of narcissistic miring in the imaginary, but by knowingly falling into that imaginary one

10. *Ecrits,* p. 12; translated by Jeffrey Mehlman in *Yale French Studies* 48 (1972), p. 41.

11. Lacan, *Ecrits* I (Paris: Seuil, Collection Points, 1970), p. 8.

has the chance of glimpsing the symbolic, of taking cognizance of translation as translation, of the mirror as mirror. Unfortunately this Franco-American seminar that would be a "natural" opener for a translation of *Ecrits* is not translated by Sheridan. As already noted, on at least one occasion Sheridan's translation works to control the anxiety produced by the double. The "Seminar" lies in wait as a mirror image for Lacan's English translator. By not translating it, Sheridan misses a chance to confront his translating as translation. He misses the chance to do a Lacanian translation and settles for merely a translation of Lacan.

The Seminar is translated by an American, Jeffrey Mehlman, who seems to have benefited from his encounter with this mirror and thus come to articulate his understanding of a certain Franco-American imaginary. In an article called "Poe Pourri," he writes: "One begins wondering then to what extent the French in idealizing Poe, have not quite simply fallen for Poe's deluded idealization of Gallic genius. More specifically and worse yet . . . in taking Lacan's text seriously . . . might we not *at best* be lapsing into Poe's delusion?"[12] Mehlman then refers to this all as a "proliferating play of mirrors." Lacan is in a long tradition of Frenchmen who have celebrated Poe's genius. Poe idealized French genius (in the person of Dupin, hero of "The Purloined Letter"). The French love the American writer because he gives them a flattering image of themselves. But this is a two-way mirror. Psychoanalytically, "idealization" always betrays a marked component of narcissism; one idealizes an object with which one identifies.[13] If Poe creates a mirror for the French, it is not the "pure mirror" of analytic neutrality, but an imaginary likeness. Poe does not reflect French imagoes, he projects his own imagoes onto the French, who accept them. Several times throughout this article Mehlman refers to Lacan's opposition to "American ego psychology"; however, he never connects that adversarial Franco-American relation to the

12. Jeffrey Mehlman, "Poe Pourri: Lacan's Purloined Letter," *Semiotexte* 1, 3 (1975), 52.
13. See Laplanche and Pontalis, *Vocabulaire*, p. 186.

positive idealized Franco-American identification that introduces and situates his article. In the Laplanche and Pontalis
article "Idealization," we read that, for Melanie Klein, "the idealization of the object would be essentially a defense against the
destructive drives; in this sense, it would be a correlative of an
extreme case of *splitting* between a 'good' object, idealized and
endowed with all the virtues . . . and a bad object whose per-
secuting character is equally carried to the limit" (pp. 186–87).
Has America thus been "split" into Poe (good object) and the
ego psychologists (bad object)? Is not Poe's relation to the
French in some way analogous to the ego psychologist's relation
to his patients? Poe offers the French a good, strong ego image.
What begins as Poe's imago, the French (including Lacan) take
on as their own.

Mehlman is promoting the new French genius Lacan, and is
thus undoubtedly repeating Poe's francophilia. But he is aware
of his repetition of Poe; he does not pretend to be immune to
delusion, but rather emphasizes his own implication in the diz-
zying structures he is describing. Mehlman also points to a way
out—"a reading of Lacan on Poe may be our best guide in
avoiding the pitfalls entailed by a reading of Lacan on Poe" (p.
52). Lacan's American reader runs the risk of belief in Lacan's
"Gallic genius." In other words, the danger is that one might
presume Lacan "knows," might produce a transference onto
Lacan. But as we have seen before, that transference is best
understood through Lacan's explanation of it. But then that
means Lacan *does* "know."

How can one distinguish between these two kinds of "knowledge," between the idealized genius product of an identificatory
francophilia, and the lucid, technical knowledge of precisely
such structures of transference? How, in Mehlman's terms, can
one distinguish between two different "reading(s) of Lacan on
Poe," between the "pitfalls" and the "guide"? Mehlman makes
such a distinction in relation to the Poe tale: "It should, moreover, be clear that to the extent that there is a locus of power in
Lacan's version of the tale, it is not in the intellectual strength of
the master-analyst Dupin, but rather in the persistence of a

structure whose mode of existence is the erosion of just such an imaginary autonomy. We are far from Poe as adolescent idealizer of otherworldly genius in the Frenchman's reading" (pp. 55–56). Mehlman accepts Lacan's distinction between Dupin's mastery (merely an illusion) and the sovereignty of a structure. In other words, it is the structure that creates the illusion of mastery; the symbolic makes the imaginary possible. With Lacan we are "far from Poe as adolescent idealizer." But, whereas at the beginning of Mehlman's article Poe worships "Gallic genius," now three pages later he idealizes "otherworldly genius." This shift makes possible the nonrecognition of a certain "play of mirrors" when Mehlman writes, "We are far from Poe as adolescent idealizer of *otherworldly genius* in *the Frenchman's* reading." Yet, if at this moment Lacan is called "the Frenchman," it serves only to remind us that the other occasion of such an appellation immediately follows the statement "A reading of Lacan on Poe may be our best guide in avoiding the pitfalls entailed by a reading of Lacan on Poe" (p. 52). I can only agree and ironically add that a reading of Mehlman on Lacan may be our best guide in avoiding the pitfalls entailed by a reading of Mehlman on Lacan. After all, when Mehlman writes that with the Frenchman "we are *far* from Poe," does not "far" belie the same imaginary belief in "otherworldly" superiority?

Mehlman's situation begins to resemble the uncanny effect Poe can produce—for example, in the story "The Black Cat," when a narrator lucidly describes his own delusion without being any less prey to that delusion. Mehlman himself asks, "Might we not *at best* be lapsing into Poe's delusion?" What is the sense of the italicized "at best"? What could be worse than this lapse? It would be worse *not* to lapse into Poe's delusion. Avoiding delusion altogether is not a possible alternative. There is no direct apprehension of the real, no possible liberation from imagoes, no unmediated reading of a text. The alternative to lapsing into Poe's delusion is lapsing into another delusion, one not shared with Poe, a delusion which is particular, idiosyncratic, and does not already have a place in Lacan's text. To the extent that we can already delineate the structure of Poe's delusion, if *that* is our delusion, we can understand it *as* delusion. Any other delusion is likely to pass as "real."

Mehlman's "lapse" sets up an identification between Lacan and Dupin, the two French geniuses admired by American idealizers. But the identification has even more substance to it. As Mehlman reminds us, Dupin is a "master-analyst." "The Purloined Letter" is the third of a trilogy of Dupin stories. "The Murders in the Rue Morgue," the first Dupin story, begins with preliminary remarks on "the mental features discoursed of as the analytical" and on the behavior of "the analyst." At the end of this prologue on "analysis," we read: "The narrative which follows will appear to the reader somewhat in the light of commentary upon the propositions just advanced. Residing in Paris during the spring and part of the summer of 18–, I there became acquainted with a Monsieur C. August Dupin." Dupin is introduced immediately after the discourse on "the analyst," and the reader can only assume that Dupin is "the analyst." The prologue has described "the analyst" as "fond of enigmas, of conundrums, of hieroglyphics; exhibiting in his solutions of each a degree of *acumen* which appears to the ordinary apprehension preternatural." Dupin certainly fits this description.

Dupin also fits the popular image of the psychoanalyst. He is clever at interpreting, at guessing what goes on inside other people's minds ("He boasted to me . . . that most men, in respect to himself, wore windows in their bosoms," the narrator says of Dupin). This Dupin bears a striking resemblance to Lacan. Both love riddles and plays on words, both display a biting contempt for the stupidity of all those positivists around them who are mired in naive delusions and incapable of seeing the "truth." In Dupin, we can recognize Lacan's flamboyant style and extreme conceit. Yet let us beware this obvious identification of Dupin with the analyst. "A little *too* self-evident," Dupin says in "The Purloined Letter," and Lacan repeats.[14] "A little *too* self-evident," Lacan says, in English, explicitly repeating Du-

---

14. *Ecrits*, p. 23; Mehlman trans., p. 53. The italics are Poe's, repeated and noted as such by Lacan.

pin's very words, broadly playing his identification with Dupin, which, the reader should be alerted, is itself a little *too* self-evident.

Dupin is not just too obvious a choice for the "analyst," but he is too "self-evident." His "self" is too evident to be the pure surface of analytic neutrality as Lacan has formulated it. On the other hand, there is the narrator whose "self" is barely evident at all. Derrida, in criticizing Lacan's lack of concern with the narrator, writes: "The narrator . . . is like the neutral, homogeneous, transparent element of the tale. He 'adds nothing,' says Lacan. As if one had to add something to intervene in a scene."[15] Derrida seems to imply ("as if . . .") that Lacan considers the narrator unimportant because Lacan says he "adds nothing." However, if anyone has formulated the effect, the "intervention" of someone who is "neutral," it is Lacan who thus describes the structure of the analyst's intervention in the transference. Through Derrida's description of the narrator as homogeneous and transparent, we can see him as "the pure mirror of an unruffled surface."

If "The Purloined Letter" functions as a parable of psychoanalysis, we must ask carefully: who is the analyst? Dupin is the "too self-evident" answer. Dupin fits the popular image of the analyst; he is the imaginary version of the analyst. But it is the neutral, nearly selfless American narrator who comes closer to functioning as an analyst.

"The Murders in the Rue Morgue" begins thus: "The mental features discoursed of as the analytical are, in themselves, but little susceptible of analysis. We appreciate them only in their effects." The narrator's problem is how to analyze analysis, how to analyze the analyst rather than be taken in by his "effects." (Psycho-) analysis, according to Lacan, is the move from the imaginary to the symbolic. Analysis produces imaginary effects (transference, projection of imagoes), but its goal is to understand what structures those effects. Is not the narrator's diffi-

15. Derrida, *La Carte postale*, p. 457; trans., p. 50.

culty (analyze the analytical) our very problem in trying to give a symbolic reading of Lacan?

A reader opens Lacan's *Ecrits,* presumably in order to learn what the "master-analyst" has to say. But thanks to Derrida's delineation of the structure of the double in "The Purloined Letter," we see that she immediately encounters the question of who is the analyst. The "too self-evident" answer is Lacan. Lacan plays a certain imaginary of the analyst to the hilt; he plays the "subject presumed to know," the great oracle, interpreter of enigmas. To fall for the illusion of Lacan's mastery is to be trapped in the imaginary of the text. In the same opening essay we are given an alternative version of the analyst in the "neutral, homogeneous, transparent" narrator. It would seem, then, that here we might find the symbolic, here we might have a chance to analyze the analytical rather than be dazzled by the "master-analyst's" flamboyant effects.

So as reader of Lacan, in my attempt to delineate the symbolic in the *Ecrits,* I find myself identifying with Poe's narrator. It is certainly to the point that in situating my reading I choose to identify with the American, not the Frenchman in the story. But more startling, and more suspect, I choose to locate "the analyst" in the American who is my double, rather than in the Gallic genius. Rather than simply presuming Lacan to know, I am presuming he presumes me to know. Might I not *at best* be lapsing into Lacan's delusion? Although I have identified the narrator with the symbolic, the fact that he is, after all, a double of Dupin and the fact that I "identify" with him (her? no real evidence to the contrary) serve as clues that this identification is an imaginary version of the symbolic.

Yet if we are to analyze the analytical, we must risk the anxiety of the double. And if there is a dialogue possible between Lacan and America, perhaps the only chance is for someone to assume the place where that dialogue is already going on, the dialogue between Dupin and his American friend. And the best that I could presume to hope for is that I might "add nothing."

3

Where to Begin?

As the preceding chapter emphasizes, Lacan's *Ecrits* begins
with the "Seminar on 'The Purloined Letter.' " Sheridan's translation, *Ecrits: A Selection*, which does not include the "Seminar,"
begins with an essay entitled "The Mirror Stage as Formative of
the Function of the I as Revealed in Psychoanalytic Experience."[1] The jacket copy to *Ecrits: A Selection* tells us that "The
Mirror Stage" is "the earliest in date" of the collection. Sheridan's selection thus appears to begin with the earliest text, as
part of a chronological order. Yet closer examination of the bibliographical information reveals a slight chronological irregularity. The jacket copy's statement that it is the earliest is there
amplified by the information that " 'The Mirror Stage' was delivered in its original form to the fourteenth International Psychoanalytical Congress in 1936." But the text translated is not the
"original form," but rather "a much revised later version" (*S,*
xiii). In fact, the essay that opens Sheridan's translation dates
from 1949, when it was delivered at the sixteenth International
Psychoanalytical Congress, and thus cannot be considered the

1. This chapter is dedicated to James Creech, whose work on prolepsis
and whose comments on "The Mirror Stage" in his article " 'Chasing after
Advances': Diderot's Article 'Encyclopedia,' " *Yale French Studies* 63 (1982),
183–97, inspired my reading of "The Mirror Stage."

earliest. The essay following it in the collection, "Aggressivity in Psychoanalysis," dates from 1948. But we cannot simply rectify chronology by reversing the order of these two essays, since the 1948 text makes reference to "The Mirror Stage."[2]

The first entry in "Bibliographical Information in Chronological Order" in the French *Ecrits* is "The Mirror Stage," but the fifth entry is "The Mirror Stage as Formative of the Function of the I." The latter entry *follows* "Aggressivity in Psychoanalysis" (*E*, 917). Sheridan condenses the two different "mirror stage" entries in his bibliographical note, at the same time making one slight alteration. He writes: "An English translation of [the 1936] version appeared in *The International Journal of Psycho-analysis,* vol. 18, part I, January, 1937, under the title, 'The Looking-glass Phase'" (*S*, p. xiii). The first entry in the French bibliography simply reads "Cf. *The International Journal of Psycho-analysis*, vol. 18, part I, January, 1937, p. 78, where this paper is inscribed under the title 'The Looking-glass Phase.'" Upon consulting the 1937 journal, one realizes that the French bibliography is not just ambiguous, but ironic. The other papers from the congress are summarized there, but one finds nothing at all *under* the title "The Looking-glass Phase." No version, no translation, not even a summary, simply the words "J. Lacan (Paris), The Looking-glass Phase."

The irony is highlighted by a footnote in the introduction to the section of *Ecrits* that contains "The Mirror Stage." In that note Lacan informs us that he "had in fact neglected to deliver the text for the report of the congress" (*E*, 67n). That same footnote directs the reader to a passage in Lacan's 1946 essay "Remarks on Mental Causality." In that essay, written before the second "Mirror Stage," he refers to the original "Mirror

2. Muller and Richardson are aware of this slight problem with chronology and find it necessary to offer reasons for ignoring this irregularity in their order of presentation: "'Aggressivity in Psychoanalysis' dates from 1948, one year before the 'Mirror Stage' essay, but since the two are cut from the same cloth and the former appears immediately after the latter in the *Selection*, we shall examine them in the order in which they appear in the English edition" (*Lacan and Language*, p. 27).

Stage," stating: "I did not give my paper to the report of the congress and you can find the essential in a few lines in my article on the family which appeared in 1938 in the *Encyclopédie française*" (*E*, 195). The reader can find "the essential," but she cannot find the original version. The original "Mirror Stage" was never published. Each entry in the French *Ecrits* bibliography corresponds to a text in *Ecrits*, except for the first. The first entry is a blind entry.

Now my point is not really or not simply to be fastidious about chronological order, but rather to point to some difficulty around the question of where to begin, some slight confusion about the "beginning" of *Ecrits*, some trouble about where (and how) to begin reading. In his book on Lacan, Jean-Michel Palmier states: "we will begin the study of the work of Jacques Lacan with the two texts that he devoted to 'The Mirror Stage' " (*Lacan*, 19). "The Mirror Stage" is the "logical," the "natural" place to begin, but, as Palmier notes, there are two "Mirror Stage" texts. A page later he distinguishes between them: "The first writing [écrit] of Lacan devoted to the Mirror Stage remains at certain points quite imprecise. The second, despite the habitual difficulties relative to the Lacanian style, is of an incomparable richness" (p. 20). For the first "écrit," Palmier gives as his footnote that 1937 *International Journal of Psycho-analysis*. Quite imprecise, at certain points, indeed!

If Palmier characterizes as quite imprecise something he in fact cannot have read, it is not only that he is covering up insufficient research, but that he considers it necessary in order to write about Lacan to read this text which cannot be read. If Palmier cannot admit to not having done so, it is because the lack of this originary text could disqualify any study of the work of Lacan. It is the first entry in the *Ecrits* bibliography. It is the origin; we must begin there. But we cannot read it, precisely. We could read "a few lines," or "the essential" in "The Family." But "the essential" is always "quite imprecise on certain points." "The Mirror Stage" is the place to begin a study of Lacan's work. Yet not only does *Ecrits* not begin there, but it turns out that "there" may be a difficult place to locate exactly, a lost origin, one might say.

In her book on Lacan, Catherine Clément writes: "Lacan, perhaps, has never *thought* anything else besides the mirror stage. . . . It is the germ containing everything [Tout y est contenu en germe]. . . . When the war comes along, Lacan's thought is formed" (*Vies et légendes*, 119; trans., 100–101). The war separates the two versions of "The Mirror Stage." Somewhere between the 1936 and the 1949 version, Lacan's thought, the thought we identify as "Lacan's," is "formed." The title of the 1949 version is "The Mirror Stage as *Formative* of the Function of the I." The essay is about the "formation," the forming of an "I," of an identity. And the text itself is formative of an identity we call Lacan. Clément says that Lacan's thought is all found there *en germe*. According to Lacan, what is formed in the mirror stage—"this form," he writes—"will be the rootstock" (*la souche*; Sheridan translates "source") of later identifications (*E*, 94; *S*, 2). If "The Mirror Stage" poses tricky bibliographical questions of origin and chronology, it is only appropriate since the essay is precisely about the origin of a chronology. And if we are having some difficulty stabilizing chronology at this origin, we will soon find that the temporality of "The Mirror Stage" is in some way alien to the logic of chronology.

A word of caution seems appropriate here. I have been so captivated by the resemblance between what Clément says *about* "the Mirror Stage" and what Lacan says *in* it, that, in my enthusiasm, I accepted, unquestioningly, if only momentarily, her claim that all Lacan is there *en germe*. Lacan, I find, has anticipated Clément's assertion. In the introduction to the section of *Ecrits* that contains "The Mirror Stage," he writes: "It happens that our students delude themselves in our writings into finding 'already there' that to which our teaching has since brought us" (*E*, 67). Clément's gesture of finding all Lacan *en germe* in the mirror stage is precisely finding "already there" what has come "since."

It is, however, difficult to read Lacan's statement about his students' self-delusions simply as an admonition against chronological infidelity. Lacan's students are reading earlier writings in view of later Lacan teachings. This implies reading what comes "after," "before," and what comes "before," "after."

Such a violation of chronological order is encouraged by *Ecrits*, which presents the 1956 "Seminar on 'The Purloined Letter'" before the earlier texts. But even more to the point, here, is an analogy between the students' illusion and the infants' "mirage" in the mirror stage. According to Lacan, in the mirror stage "the subject anticipates in a mirage the maturation of his power" (*E*, 94–95; *S*, 2). The student anticipates in the early texts the maturation of Lacan's teachings. Thus, somehow, the effect of Lacan's text on his students is analogous to the effect of the mirror on the infant. Lacan's text functions as an illusory mirror image. So we find structures of transference onto his text similar to those discussed in the preceding chapter.

I said above that Clément's *en germe* claim produced an enthusiasm in me, which immediately became embarrassing. My embarrassment corresponded to a realization that it was extremely pleasurable to find the later Lacan "already there" in the early writing. An anticipation of maturation produced joy along with a willingness to suspend disbelief. This joy may resemble the "jubilation" Lacan ascribes to the child assuming his mirror image, being captivated by an analogy and suspending his disbelief.

Briefly: in the mirror stage, the infant who has not yet mastered the upright posture and who is supported by either another person or some prosthetic device will, upon seeing herself in the mirror, "jubilantly assume" the upright position. She thus finds in the mirror image "already there," a mastery that she will actually learn only later. The jubilation, the enthusiasm, is tied to the temporal dialectic by which she appears *already* to be what she will *only later become*.

The temporal dialectic in which Lacan's students are enmeshed is not exactly one of anticipation, of seeing the future in the present. Both the "present" and the "future" here are actually "pasts." The students read the past in light of a more recent past, read early Lacan writings in light of more recent Lacan teachings. Indeed one might be tempted to contrast the infant's anticipation with the students' retroaction. But it turns out that the mirror stage itself is both an anticipation and a retroaction.

The mirror stage is a turning point. After it, the subject's relation to himself is always mediated through a totalizing image that has come from outside. For example, the mirror image becomes a totalizing ideal that organizes and orients the self. But since the "self" is necessarily a totalized, unified concept—a division between an inside and an outside—there is no "self" before the mirror stage. The mirror stage is thus a turning point, but between what and what? It is a turning point in the chronology of a self, but it is also the origin, the moment of constitution of that self. What therefore precedes it?

According to Palmier, "what seems to be first . . . is the anguish of the *corps morcelé* [body in bits and pieces]" (p. 23). The *corps morcelé* is a Lacanian term for a violently nontotalized body image, an image psychoanalysis finds accompanied by anxiety. In the mirror stage the formation of the first self is based on the first totalized image of the body: totalized rather than in bits and pieces. Although Palmier says that the anguish of the *corps morcelé* "seems to be first," implying that this may be merely appearance and that something else may actually be first, the rest of his presentation of the mirror stage treats the anteriority of the "anguish of the body in bits and pieces" as a certainty: for example, "[the mirror stage] is a drama that sees the anticipated image of the body as totality replace the anguish of the body in bits and pieces" (p. 22). Palmier is not alone; this is the generally understood notion of the mirror stage: a turning point where the "body in bits and pieces" becomes a totalized body image, a proto-self.

In the article "The Mirror Stage" of *The Language of Psychoanalysis*, Jean Laplanche and Jean-Baptiste Pontalis explain "the body in bits and pieces" and "the mirror stage" in Freudian terms. The former would correspond to a primordial, polymorphous autoerotic state that is prior to the constitution of the ego and therefore of narcissism proper (as opposed to autoerotism). Narcissism is love of an image of self, and so demands the image of self which is achieved for the first time in the mirror stage. Laplanche and Pontalis thus *seem to answer* that the body in bits and pieces precedes the mirror stage. But they then add:

"Except for one important nuance: for Lacan, it would be the mirror stage which would *retroactively* bring forth the phantasy of the body in bits and pieces."[3] The mirror stage would *seem to come after* "the body in bits and pieces" and organize them into a unified image. But actually, *that* violently unorganized *image only comes after* the mirror stage so as to *represent what came before.* What appears to precede the mirror stage is simply a projection or a reflection. There is nothing on the other side of the mirror.

There is something quite difficult about the temporal order of the mirror stage. It produces contradictions in those trying to describe it. For example, in her book on Lacan, Angèle Kremer-Marietti writes: "This drama is thus the manifest proof that the unity of the body, far from being given and first, is acquired through anguishing vicissitudes beginning with the vision of a body in bits and pieces and moving on to the certainty of an exterior form [*Gestalt*], restoring [*restitutrice de*] the totality of the body."[4] According to this sentence, unity is not first but follows from "the vision of a body in bits and pieces." The *corps morcelé* is first, but. . . . Then Kremer-Marietti calls the "exterior form" not *constitutrice* (constitutive) but *"restitutrice* of the totality." If the totality which is acquired in the mirror stage is not, at that moment, constituted but rather restored, it must have been present earlier and then disappeared. If the *Gestalt* "restores" a totality, then some totality, some unity must have preceded the body in bits and pieces. Without explicitly confronting the problematic temporality of the mirror stage, we are led to contradiction: the unity is not first, but at the same time it must have preceded the vision of the body in bits and pieces.

The mirror stage is a decisive moment. Not only does the self issue from it, but so does "the body in bits and pieces." This moment is the source not only for what follows but also for what precedes. It produces the future through anticipation and the

3. Laplanche and Pontalis, *Vocabulaire de la psychanalyse,* p. 453, italics mine.

4. Angèle Kremer-Marietti, *Lacan et la rhétorique de l'inconscient* (Paris: Aubier-Montaigne, 1978), p. 87.

past through retroaction. And yet it is itself a moment of self-delusion, of captivation by an illusory image. Both future and past are thus rooted in an illusion.

Lacan and his commentators have emphasized the illusion in the mirror stage. It is the founding moment of the imaginary mode, the belief in a projected image. It represents the first instance of what according to Lacan is the basic function of the ego, the classic gesture of the self: *méconnaissance*, misprision, misrecognition. According to Lacan, "the important point is that [the ideal formed in the mirror stage] situates the agency of the *ego* . . . in a line of fiction" (*E*, 94; *S*, 2). That may be "the important point," but I would like to emphasize not the fictionality so much as the temporal dialectic of a moment that is at once anticipatory and retroactive.

Both anticipation and retroaction are violations of chronology, but separately either can, if necessary, be sorted out, their elements reassigned to their proper chronological place. The specific difficulty in thinking the temporality of the mirror stage is its intrication of anticipation and retroaction. The retroaction is based on the anticipation. In other words, the self is constituted through anticipating what it will become, and then this anticipatory model is used for gauging what was before.

As I noted earlier, Lacan writes that what is formed in the mirror stage "will be the rootstock of secondary identifications" (*E*, 94; *S*, 2). "Will be" is an anticipatory gesture, but what is anticipated is that "this form" will have been the "rootstock," that is, the necessary antecedent to the later identifications. Only by an effect of retroaction from the anticipated identifications do we understand that what happens in the mirror stage is the formation of a "rootstock." What thus occurs in the mirror stage is the formation of what in the future will be an antecedent, what grammatically can be called a "future perfect," the formation of what *will have been* a rootstock. Later, in the famous "Discours de Rome," Lacan will have written: "what realizes itself in my history is not the past definite of what was since it is no longer, nor even the present perfect of what has been in what I am, but the future perfect of what I will have been for what I am in the process of becoming."[5] "My history," subjective history, the history of a subject, is a succession of future perfects, pasts of a future, moments twice removed from "present reality" by the combined action of an anticipation and a retroaction.

In the introduction to the section of *Ecrits* in which we find "The Mirror Stage," Lacan writes: "We thus find ourselves putting these texts back in a future perfect: they will have anticipated our insertion of the unconscious in language" (*E*, 71). The future perfect is the time of what Lacan will have called "my history," in this case specifically "Lacan's history," what Lacan will have been for what he (in 1953, in the "Discours de Rome") is in the process of becoming. The *Ecrits* is the history of his thought, by and large presented in chronological order. And in 1966 as he writes the introduction to the "Mirror Stage" section, that text is, retroactively, put back in a future perfect, where it will have anticipated, for example, the "Discours de Rome." The time of the *Ecrits* is a future perfect.

Yet the chronology of the sentence from the introduction is further complicated. In 1966 Lacan retroactively sees that these texts anticipate: the retroaction precedes and makes possible the anticipation. But the retroaction puts the texts back into a future perfect, which is a tense in which an anticipation (of the future) precedes a retroaction (of what is anterior to that anticipated future). If in this sentence it seems particularly difficult to determine which comes first—anticipation or retroaction—perhaps it is because the intrication of the two, which seems to accompany the mirror stage on every level, renders radically difficult the question of what comes first. Where to begin?

In "The Mirror Stage," Lacan writes that "this development is lived like a temporal dialectic that decisively projects the formation of the individual into history" (*E*, 97; *S*, 4). "Development," "lived," and "formation" imply a natural progression, a succes-

5. "The Function and Field of Speech and Language in Psychoanalysis" in *Ecrits*, p. 300; *Ecrits: A Selection*, p. 86. Also translated by Anthony Wilden in *The Language of the Self*.

sion of present or past moments. But the mirror stage is "decisive." It is a turning point that "projects" the individual into "history," that is into the future perfect. The individual is no longer living a natural development, a chronological maturation. She is projected, thrown forward, in an anticipation that makes her progress no longer a natural development but a "history," a movement doubly twisted by anticipation and retroaction. Yet the difficulty in thinking the temporality of the mirror stage is that it is nonetheless a moment *in the* natural maturation *process*, a moment which projects the individual *out of that process*. It is the moment in a chronology that violates that very order. As Lacan writes: "It is the moment that decisively . . . makes of the *I* that apparatus for which every push of the instincts will be a danger, even should it correspond to a natural maturation" (*E*, 98; *S*, 5).

Lacan earlier says that the infant "anticipates the maturation of his power." Yet now we see that the anticipation is much more complicated than a simple projection into a future. For the anticipated maturation will never simply arrive. Not that the infant will not learn to walk, grow up, become capable of independent survival. But the very process of "natural maturation" is now affected by the anticipation. It at first appears that the infant is inscribed in an inevitable developmental chronology and merely "anticipates" a later moment in that development, but the "I," the subject primordially formed in the mirror stage, the subject that can say "my history," must defend against "natural maturation," must defend against natural chronology in favor of the future perfect. Any "natural maturation" simply proves that the self was not mature before, and since the self was founded upon an assumption of maturity, the discovery that maturity was prematurely assumed is the discovery that the self is built on hollow ground. Since the entire past and present is dependent upon an already anticipated maturity—that is, a projected ideal one—any "natural maturation" (however closely it might resemble the anticipated ideal one) must be defended against, for it threatens to expose the fact that the self is an illusion done with mirrors.

Just as the subject cannot simply mature, cannot advance into the future that he anticipated as his birthright, neither can he inalienably possess his past. He can never simply fall back on some accomplishment, rest on some laurels already won, since the "past" itself is based upon a future that is necessarily an uncertainty. Not that he will have done nothing, or will simply have forgotten what happened, but the significance of his past is dependent upon revelation in the future, and it is only as significant experience that any past can be "his past," his experience, the accomplishment of a subject.

Lacan finally did get a paper published in *The International Journal of Psycho-analysis*—not in 1937, but in 1953. In that article, he writes: "This illusion of unity, in which a human being is always looking forward to self-mastery, entails a constant danger of sliding back again into the chaos from which he started; it hangs over the abyss of a dizzy Ascent in which one can perhaps see the very essence of Anxiety."[6] The "maturation of his power" which the infant anticipated now has a new name: "self-mastery." Yet the "self" that must be mastered is the product of an anticipatory illusion. To "master" the self, to understand it, would be to realize its falsity, and therefore the impossibility of coinciding with one's self. The moment of "self-mastery" cannot but be infinitely deferred. But that moment would also be the revelation of the meaning of the past (the future perfect), and so the acquisition and comprehension of the past are also infinitely deferred. No ground is ever definitively covered, and one always risks sliding all the way back. Hence the effect of anticipation is anxiety. But how can we correlate this anxiety with the infant's jubilation, equally an effect of anticipation?

In *Inhibitions, Symptoms and Anxiety*, Freud writes, "the id cannot have anxiety as the ego can; for it is not an organization."[7] Anxiety may, then, be connected to organization. That which is

6. Jacques Lacan, "Some Reflections on the Ego," *International Journal of Psycho-analysis* 34 (1953), 15.

7. Sigmund Freud, *Inhibitions, Symptoms and Anxiety*, S.E. xx, 140.

not organized or totalized or unified cannot be violated. The anxiety that Lacan represents as the risk of "sliding back again into . . . chaos" can be experienced only by the ego with its "illusion of unity." But the mirror stage is only the first step in the "dizzy Ascent." At this point the subject can "look forward" without the fear of "sliding back," since she is just beginning her climb. The ego is only just being formed and as yet has no ongoing organization to be endangered. The mirror stage is a fleeting moment of jubilation before an inevitable anxiety sets in.

The mirror stage is thus high tragedy: a brief moment of doomed glory, a paradise lost. The infant is "decisively projected" out of this joy into the anxious defensiveness of "history," much as Adam and Eve are expelled from paradise into the world. Just as man and woman are already created but do not enter the human condition until expelled from Eden, so the child, although already born, does not become a self until the mirror stage. Both cases are two-part birth processes: once born into "nature," the second time into "history." When Adam and Eve eat from the tree of knowledge, they anticipate mastery. But what they actually gain is a horrified recognition of their nakedness. This resembles the movement by which the infant, having assumed by anticipation a totalized, mastered body, then retroactively perceives his inadequacy (his "nakedness"). Lacan has written another version of the tragedy of Adam and Eve.

If the mirror stage is a lost paradise, it is appropriate to recall that the text "The Mirror Stage" is likewise a lost, originary moment. And perhaps the bibliographical thinking done earlier can help us work through this tragedy. There are, you will recall, two "Mirror Stages"—one not in print, an oral event lost to recorded history; the other readily available, frequently reprinted, translated, collected. This doubling, however, undermines the uniqueness of the original, lost version. For example, in Palmier's study and in Sheridan's translation, the loss is forgotten, covered over in various ways. If the paradise that is lost is not unique, then it is not exactly lost. In just such a way, perhaps, the jubilation of originary anticipation need not be lost.

Lacan does not term the mirror stage a tragedy, but he does call it a "drama." "The mirror stage is a drama whose internal impetus lunges forward [*se précipiter*, precipitates itself] from insufficiency to anticipation—and which, for the subject captivated by the lure of spatial identification, machinates the succession of fantasies which go from an image of the body in bits and pieces to a form which we will call orthopedic of its totality—and to the armor finally assumed of an alienating identity, which will mark with its rigid structure his entire mental development" (*E*, 97; *S*, 4). This precipitous internal impetus is the ineluctable unfolding of a drama. The child's destiny is sealed: insufficiency (body in bits and pieces) to anticipation (orthopedic form) and "finally" to a rigid armor. But let us carefully examine the chronology implicit here. The infant is thrown forward from "insufficiency" to "anticipation." However, that "insufficiency" can be understood only from the perspective of the "anticipation." The image of the body in bits and pieces is fabricated retroactively from the mirror stage. It is only the anticipated "orthopedic" form of its totality that can define—retroactively—the body as insufficient. Thus the impetus of the drama turns out to be so radically accelerated that the second term precedes the first—a precipitousness comparable to the speed of light. In this light, we must question the "finally" of the "alienating identity." In a temporal succession where the second term can precede the first, what is the status of a "finally"? By separating anticipation from retroaction, Lacan presents a tragedy. But having found that anticipation is always entangled with retroaction, we must question this tragic view. Is the "rigid armor" an inevitable conclusion?

The problem of rigidity seems to be linked to a certain sort of temporal succession, an irreversible chronology that one might call "tragic." It appears that the internal linear progression of the drama leads to rigidity. But given the effect of retroaction, one might also say that it is rigidity that produces irreversible chronology.

In Lacanian tragedy, the ego finally becomes rigid, becomes a painful, encumbering armor that constricts the psyche. The notion of rigidity also appears when Freud is discussing the ego. But with Freud it is not the ego that is rigid, but our concept of the ego. The third chapter of *Inhibitions, Symptoms and Anxiety* begins thus: "To return to the problem of the ego. The apparent contradiction is due to our having taken abstractions too rigidly" (p. 97). Freud finds he has contradicted himself from one moment to the next in his description of the ego. Rather than consider the contradiction a shortcoming, he decides that it is the overly sharp delimitation of the boundaries of the concept of the ego that causes the contradiction.

When Freud writes "the problem of the ego," we read it as our problem in conceptualizing the ego, but perhaps we might also read it as "the ego's problem." The "abstraction" that is too rigid here is our conception of the ego. But, according to Lacan's notion of the formation of the ego in "The Mirror Stage," the "self itself" is an idealized form, abstracted from the "real." So we could say that not only the psychoanalytic concept of the ego but the ego itself is too rigid an abstraction. Rigid abstraction is intrinsically "the problem of the ego."

Psychoanalytic science is engaged in the same dilemma as its object, the psyche. Rigidity is the tragedy that awaits both. Yet Freud seems to glimpse a happy ending. Not for the psyche: his outlook there is as bleak as Lacan's. But for the science. Freud is optimistic about the possibility of a science that would not be irreparably hampered by the rigidity of its concepts. If we take the liberty of seeing an analogy between the rigid concept and the rigid ego, then perhaps Freud's description of a healthy science can be helpful in finding a way for the self to sidestep its inevitable progress to rigidity.

Freud is addressing the question of "where to begin"—our question in this chapter. Where does Lacan's *Ecrits* begin? Where does a science begin? Freud's discussion of this question begins the article called "Instincts and Their Vicissitudes": "The view is often defended that sciences should be built up on clear and sharply defined basal concepts. In actual fact no science, not even the most exact, begins with such definitions. The true beginning of scientific activity consists in describing phenomena and then in proceeding to group, classify, and correlate them."[8] It is interesting that the "defense" ("is often defended") is associated with the priority of "clear and sharply defined" concepts. The clear and sharp definition recalls the orthopedic, organized, ideal form of the self, anticipated in the mirror stage. As we have seen, it is precisely this clearly defined form that leads to defensiveness, to "armor." Freud contrasts the defended view (the defensive ideal) with "actual fact," asserting that science actually begins with description and not definition. He thus appears to have answered the chronological question "Where does science begin?".

But he goes on:

> Even at the stage of description it is not possible to avoid applying certain abstract ideas to the material in hand, ideas derived from various sources and certainly not the fruit of new experience only. Such ideas—which will later become the basal concepts of the science—are still more indispensible as the material is further elaborated. They must at first necessarily possess some measure of uncertainty; there can be no question of any clear delimitation of their content. So long as they remain in this condition, we come to an understanding about their meaning by repeated references to the material of observation, from which we seem to have deduced our abstract ideas, but which is in point of fact subject to them.

The "true beginning" is description. However, the "true beginning," untainted by abstraction, turns out to be itself only an abstraction. In actual fact, abstraction is unavoidable, even at

8. Sigmund Freud, "Instincts and Their Vicissitudes," *S.E.* xiv, 117. My quotations from this article modify the *Standard Edition* translation following the translation by Cecil M. Baines that appears in Sigmund Freud, *General Psychological Theory*, ed. Philip Rieff (New York: Collier, 1963), pp. 83–84. Lacan quotes this passage at length in one of his published seminars. See also Samuel Weber, *The Legend of Freud* (Minneapolis: University of Minnesota Press, 1982), pp. 33–34.

the stage of description, even though these abstractions do not derive from "new experience." Yet these abstractions are not yet concepts; they "will later become the basal concepts." The base, the foundation is not laid first; it will be built later, retroactively. These abstractions are anticipations of retroactive basal concepts—very much as the image of the self formed in the mirror stage "will be the rootstock."

Then Freud comes to a slight irregularity. The abstractions "seem" to follow the "material of observation"; but in fact that material follows the "abstract ideas." Again a comparison with the mirror stage is enlightening. Lacan says that the "total form of the body . . . is more constitutive than constituted" (E, 94–95; S, 2). By this I understand that, although it seems that the image of one's own body as total form is deduced from "the material of observation," from what the child observes in the mirror, in point of fact the total form is an abstract idea that shapes the observation. The question of which comes first—abstract idea or observation; image of one's body as total form or perception of one's body as total form—remains tricky to answer.

It is perhaps the uncertainty of the answer to this question which offers the most hope. So long as the concepts remain to some degree uncertain, that is, flexible, not sharply defined, not rigidly armored, then the question need not be answered. We can "come to an understanding"—things go well; we can get along. There is an exchange, "repeated references" between the abstractions and the observations. Since there is a repeated back and forth movement, priority is not particularly important.

"Thus, strictly speaking," Freud continues, "they are in the nature of conventions; although everything depends on their being chosen in no arbitrary manner, but determined by the important relations they have to the empirical material—relations that we seem to divine before we can clearly recognize and demonstrate them." The concepts are conventions; which is to say, they are fictions. Not only that, but they are "divined": they are anticipatory projections. The analogy to the mirror stage dynamic is evident. For Lacan and the infant subject this building upon a fiction is tragic; whereas for Freud and the infant science, likewise constructing upon fictional foundations, there is hope. Somehow the avoidance of tragedy depends upon a retroactive effect reversing the internal impetus that lunges forward, a retroactive acceptance of one's foundations (whether concepts or self) as fiction. Such an acceptance might mean an openness to revision, rather than a rigid defense against the recognition of fictionality.

Freud concludes his developmental history of an infant science: "It is only after a more searching investigation of the field in question that we are able to formulate with increased clarity the scientific concepts underlying it, and progressively so to modify these concepts that they become widely applicable and at the same time consistent logically. Then, indeed, it may be time to immure them in definitions. The progress of science, however, demands a certain elasticity even in these definitions."

Here, finally, Freud seems to go beyond the strange yet now familiar temporality of the "divined" basal concepts into a one-way irreversible progression that finally "immures" the definitions. The immurement of the concepts like the armoring of the ego would definitely (definitionally?) end the more fluid interplay of anticipation and retroaction ("repeated references") that precedes it. Science would then proceed to containment, imprisonment, what I have earlier called tragedy.

If tragedy demands an irreversible chronology, then the tragic loss of elasticity in a science would be based upon a simple chronological progression in which past discoveries have become givens and present observations and theorizations are founded upon that immutable past, either accepting it or rejecting it, but never questioning that it is already known. Such doomed science would have an objective history of pasts and present perfects rather than a subjective history of future perfects.

Lacan has frequently called his contribution to psychoanalytic science, a "return to Freud." This "return" is not a simple regression back to a stable point earlier along a set line of development. It is a retroactive effect of Lacan's teachings. Reading

Freud after having read Lacan is unlike reading Freud before. Although Lacanian theory is founded upon Freud, follows Freud, the Freud that it follows is shaped, "constituted," by Lacan's reading. The question of which comes first, Freud or Lacan, although chronologically absurd, becomes a valid question.

In 1958, in "The Signification of the Phallus," Lacan will "claim that Freud's discovery takes on its value precisely in that it *must have anticipated* the formulas [of modern linguistic analysis]."[9] "Mature" Lacanian psychoanalysis will draw upon modern linguistic analysis (Ferdinand de Saussure, Roman Jakobson) which Freud could not know. But Lacan retroactively sees Freud as having "anticipated" this sort of analysis. Freud's text, in a sense, constitutes, for Lacan, the mirror stage of psychoanalytic science. In the case of the ego, the infant may jubilate, but Lacan, the tragic chorus, lucidly foretells the coming doom. But in the drama of psychoanalysis, it is not Freud but Lacan himself who jubilates retroactively at Freud's "anticipation" of "mature" psychoanalytic theory. Just as Lacan's students will retroactively enjoy reading an anticipation into his early texts.

Although Lacan may be tragic about the prognosis for the ego, the ego might look to his history of psychoanalysis for hope. After all, it is most likely there that *his* ego is to be found. It is there that Lacan is at work trying to undo irreversible rigidification. In the drama of psychoanalytic history, Lacan is not a passive, wise, ironic chorus, but a protagonist struggling against the tragic fate of immurement. This struggle against the ineluctable progress of chronology must stake its hopes upon the combined effects of anticipation and retroaction.

The question of which text comes first, Freud or Lacan, this question of a chronology of reading (rather than of writing) returns us to the question that began this chapter: where (and how) to begin reading Lacan? On one level that will always have been the implicit question of this chapter, perhaps even the

9. Jacques Lacan, "The Signification of the Phallus" in *Ecrits*, p. 688; *Ecrits: A Selection*, p. 284; *Feminine Sexuality*, p. 78; italics mine.

principal question of the present book, which is meant as an introduction to Lacan. This book is written . . . (This book will have been written—as I write of the "present" book I find the future perfect to be the most correct tense for my anticipation of your reading.) This book will have been written for people who have read Lacan's texts, and can most fully be understood as a response to Lacan. At the same time the "present" book is meant to be an enticement and an orientation for a future reading of Lacan. If I were asked to suggest to my reader which should be read first, I would want to reply: both.

And so this book which is presently (that is, in the future perfect) attempting to form itself, to create a cohesive image out of chaos, finds itself participating in the same temporal dialectic it is describing. As I thus recognize my chapter as a mirror image of itself, I am jubilant.

4

Directions for a Return to Freud

The subject of this chapter is the paper called "The Freudian Thing," which dates from 1955, the same year as "The Seminar on 'The Purloined Letter.'" Following my detour back into "The Mirror Stage," the present chapter constitutes a return to the proper time frame of this book. The direction of this return is slightly confusing, however. A return is generally a going back; yet in this case the detour was already a going back, so that the return is a coming forward once again. The encounter with the mirror reversed our directions, as mirrors are wont to do. In fact, as we saw, "The Mirror Stage" rather seriously calls into question any sense of progression or regression in relation to movement through time.

The question of a return engages us here, since the full title of the essay is "The Freudian Thing or the Meaning of the Return to Freud in Psychoanalysis." As to the meaning of this return, Lacan states: "The meaning of a return to Freud is a return to the meaning of Freud" (*E*, 405; *S*, 117). The pleasing elegance of that sentence stems from the use of the rhetorical figure chiasmus: that is, the inversion of the second of two parallel structures. The second part of the sentence is like a mirror image of the first. The pleasing compactness, the neat framing of this sentence affords the pleasure of a mirror image, the pleasure Lacan calls jubilation in "The Mirror Stage." But the mirror does not simply return a neatly framed repetition, it inverts the image, reverses the order. This sentence equates its two parts with the verb "is," implying that the order does not matter at all, What, then, is a return, what is the direction of a return, how does one direct a return if the order does not matter?

The word "meaning" in the phrase "meaning of the return to Freud" is the French word *sens*, which also commonly means "direction." It would seem that Lacan is trying to ascertain directional coordinates: the first section of the text is called "Situation in Time and Place of This Exercise." There is apparently a danger of becoming disoriented, going astray, and getting lost. The chiasmatic sentence reads "the meaning of *a* return to Freud" whereas the subtitle is "the meaning of *the* return to Freud." The divergence in articles reminds us that there can be more than one sort of return. One return returns to Freud's meaning: others may not.

How, then, to avoid losing one's way? At the end of this lecture, Lacan says of ego psychology that it is "disoriented [*désorientée*]" (*E*, 434, *S*, 143).[1] Perhaps the problem with modern psychoanalysis is that it is literally "dis-oriented," that it has turned away from the East.

In 1939 Freud, fleeing the Nazis, emigrates from Vienna to London. His westward migration is made possible by the intervention of Marie Bonaparte, who in 1953 will throw her considerable influence with the International Psychoanalytic Association against the affiliation of the newly formed Société Française de Psychanalyse. The Second World War is responsible not only for Freud's move to London but for the emigration of large numbers of psychoanalysts to America, among them Rudolf Loewenstein, not only one of the formulators of ego psychology but Lacan's former analyst. In July 1953, when Lacan is preparing to go to the Eighteenth International Psychoanalytic Con-

1. "Let it be here understood that our critique of the analysis which claims to be the analysis of resistance and which finds itself more and more reduced to the mobilization of defenses, only bears on the fact that it is as disoriented [Sheridan unfortunately writes "disorientated"] in its practice as in its principles so as to call it back to the order of its legitimate ends."

gress in London, he is informed that, because of the split with the Sociéte Psychanalytique de Paris, he is no longer a member of the international association and cannot attend the meeting. In November 1955, then, when the center of psychoanalysis has moved decidedly westward, Lacan goes from Paris to Vienna and delivers a paper whose subtitle is "The Direction [*Sens*] of the Return to Freud in Psychoanalysis."

In this paper, he glosses at length the penultimate sentence of the thirty-first of Freud's *New Introductory Lectures*. In German that sentence reads "Wo Es war, soll Ich werden," which the English Standard Edition renders as "Where id was, there ego shall be."[2] Freud's sentence is about the orientation of a return: something shall be, is obligated to be, in the same place where something was in the past. But it is a strange return, for although it is a return to the same place, it is a return by a different subject. Perhaps like the return to Vienna—accomplished not by Freud, who was there, but by Lacan, who feels the obligation to be there.

His gloss points out that the words "Es" and "Ich," contrary to Freud's usual practice, are not accompanied by the article *das*. Without articles these words are closer to their common German meanings as third and first person pronouns than they are to Freudian terminology. We might translate as "Where it was, there I ought to be." Spoken by Lacan, then: "Where it (Freudian psychoanalysis) was going on, there I shall, in the sense of a compulsion, be."

Lacan comes finally to translate this sentence as "La où c'était . . . c'est mon devoir que je vienne à être," which Sheridan translates as "There where it was . . . it is my duty that I should come to being" (*E*, 417–18; *S*, 129). Lacan takes great pains to explain his choices for the various elements of this translation, all except one. He chooses to translate "soll Ich" by the rather awkward verbiage "it is my duty that I" ("*c'est mon devoir que je*"). Earlier in this gloss he translates it by the more

2. Sigmund Freud, *New Introductory Lectures on Psycho-analysis*, S.E. XXII, 80. It is regrettable that the vagaries of usage of the English word "shall" obscure the obligation implied in the German "soll." The sentence is clearly not about simple futurity but rather concerns compulsion.

economical and more obvious "dois-je" ("I ought"), and he makes no comment as to why he does not retain this simpler version. Besides its emphasis on duty, the longer translation has another effect, one that is lost in translation to English. The longer construction demands that the verb "come" in the phrase "come to being" appear in the subjunctive, whereas with "dois je" the verb "come" would be in the infinitive. The first person singular subjunctive form compelled to emerge here is "vienne," an exact homonym of the French name for the city Freud left in 1939, in which Lacan comes to be in 1955.

We can read in Lacan's version of Freud's words, in Lacan's repeating Freud's words there where Freud himself had written them, something else that is being said. Someone is saying "mon devoir: Vienne," "my duty: Vienna." But just what or where is Vienna? Let us not be so sure we know.

In the very first sentence of "The Freudian Thing" Lacan calls Vienna "the eternal place of Freud's discovery, if one can say that through [this discovery] the true center of the human being is henceforth no longer in the same place assigned to it by an entire humanist tradition" (*E,* 401; *S,* 114). Vienna is the eternal place, "if," on the condition that, one can say something else is no longer where it has been considered to be. The stability of Vienna's location is linked to the dislocation of a center whose place our tradition has taken for granted. What eternally goes on in Vienna is the discovery that something is not where it is supposed to be.

Freud's discovery, as Lacan casts it, is that the center of the human being is not the ego, as we have long supposed, but what Lacan calls the subject, which sometimes but not always corresponds to what Freud called the id. In his seminar of May 12, 1955, Lacan states that "the present orientation of analysis is to install the ego in the center of the perspective."[3] The present orientation is thus disoriented; "Freud's discovery" has been lost. If Vienna is the eternal site of that discovery, and if that

3. Jacques Lacan, *Le Séminaire* II: *Le moi dans la théorie de Freud et dans la technique de la psychanalyse* (Paris: Seuil, 1978). p. 243. This book will henceforth be referred to in the text as *S* II.

discovery can be lost, then Vienna must not be as easy to locate as we might assume.

The dislocation is more radical than first appears. In his seminar of February 16, 1955, attempting to correct one of his students' misdirection, Lacan insists that "the subject must never be represented anywhere" (*S* II, 143). Not that the subject is nowhere, but its whereabouts cannot be mapped. In his gloss of "Wo Es war, soll Ich werden," Lacan takes the liberty of leaning upon the homonymy between "Es" and the initial letter of the word "subject." In later schemas, he will represent the subject with a capital S, to be read "Es." Thus the duty is that "I come to be" where the subject was. But since the subject's whereabouts cannot be mapped, this obligatory return trip becomes difficult indeed. Small wonder, then, that a return could get disoriented.

"To install the ego in the center of the perspective," says Lacan, "as is done in the present orientation of analysis, is only one of those returns [*retours*] to which any calling into question of man's position finds itself exposed" (*S* II, 243). Freud's discovery calls into question man's position, and finds itself exposed to the danger of a return. Yet Lacan would save the discovery precisely by means of a return. The word "retour" is the same Lacan uses for his own enterprise. Evidently, one can return in the wrong direction.

In "The Freudian Thing," he declares that American psychoanalysts' betrayal of Freudian doctrine "is to return [*faire retour*] to the reactionary principle that covers over the duality of the one who suffers and the one who heals with the opposition between the one who knows and the one who does not" (*E*, 403; *S*, 115). In other words, American psychoanalysts believe that the imaginary projections, the effects of transference which make the patient presume the analyst knows, are true. In the terms of my first chapter, they believe that the analyst is Dupin, the genius who knows the answer to all enigmas. Lacan considers this error a return to a "reactionary principle." "Reactionary" has the general sense of opposed to progress and in favor of a return to an earlier state. A return to a reactionary principle thus returns to a principle of returning.

Both Lacan's activity and that of his adversaries are "returns."

One returns to Freud's discovery; the other turns back to what preceded that discovery, to what that discovery turned away from. This dynamic in which two opposing forces are both returns to earlier states finds a striking analogy in *Beyond the Pleasure Principle*, the text that is a major point of reference for Lacan's return to Freud. It is generally understood that this strange text of 1920 results in the polar opposition of Eros and Thanatos—that is, respectively, the life instincts and the death instincts—as the two great forces in the psyche, and that it begins with a consideration of something Freud calls the "Wiederholungszwang," the repetition compulsion. But what is less clear is the interrelation between repetition and these two conflicting forces.

In the fifth chapter of *Beyond the Pleasure Principle*, Freud hypothesizes that all instincts "tend towards the restoration of an earlier state of things."[4] What concerns us here is how he goes on to articulate the difference between one sort of restorative instinct, one sort of drive to return, and another. The sexual instincts, Freud says, "are conservative in the same sense as the other instincts in that they bring back earlier states of living substance" (p. 40). The death instincts seek to return life to the inorganic stage which preceded it. It seems, then, that the difference between Eros and Thanatos is that, while both seek to return to an earlier state, the state Thanatos seeks is earlier than that sought by Eros. Thanatos wishes to return to a state preceding life itself, one that therefore totally undoes the organism.

One might venture to compare Eros/Thanatos to the two opposing forces in psychoanalysis. Lacan seeks to return to an earlier state of psychoanalysis, but one that is still recognizable as such, one that presupposes the "birth" of psychoanalysis, Freud's discovery. Ego psychology, on the other hand, seeks to return psychoanalysis to a pre-Freudian state, one in which the conscious "autonomous" ego is the center of the human psyche.

This analogy is very tempting. Let us compare. Freud writes:

4. Sigmund Freud, *Beyond the Pleasure Principle*, S.E. xvIII, 37–38. The word "instinct" translates Freud's "Trieb," which might be more correctly rendered by "drive."

The attributes of life were at some time evoked in inanimate matter . . . . The tension which then arose in what had hitherto been an inanimate substance endeavoured to cancel itself out. In this way the first instinct came into being: the instinct to return to the inanimate state. [*S.E.,* XVIII, 38]

Lacan writes:

To install the ego in the center of the perspective . . . is only one of those returns to which any calling into question of man's position finds itself exposed . . . . the proper sense of each of these revisions [of the discourse on man] is always deadened [*amorti*] in the course of time, attenuated, such that presently as always the word humanism is a sack in which there is quietly rotting, piled one on top of another, the corpses of these successive upheavals of a revolutionary point of view on man. [*S* II, 243]

Any revision in the traditional notion of man is doomed to death through a mechanism so automatic we might call it inherent, if not instinctive. That which "attenuates" in Lacan's model is like that which endeavours to cancel out "tension" in Freud's. Ego psychology is "only one of those returns" that in Freud's terms we would call a death instinct.

But I do not want to yield too quickly to this analogy. First, I would like to take into account the fact that the relation between Eros and Thanatos is more complicated than simple opposition, good guys versus bad. Freud's description of this opposition is remarkably confusing and contradictory. I choose to assume that his confusion is not simply bad thinking or bad writing but a response to the paradoxical nature of what he is attempting to describe.

One contradiction in Freud's description concerns the nature of the sexual instincts. First Freud says that "they bring back earlier states of living substance." Then, in the next paragraph he asks, "Is it really the case that, *apart from the sexual instincts,* there are no instincts that do not seek to restore an earlier state of things?" (p. 41), to which he replies affirmatively. The question implies that the sexual instincts do *not* seek to restore an earlier state. The italics in the question are Freud's, and a translator's footnote informs us that the italics were added in the second edition of the book and retained in all succeeding editions. Freud does revise his confusing text. Rather than straighten out the contradiction, he underlines it.

It is right in between these two contradictory statements that Freud first states that the sexual instincts "are the true life instincts" and that they operate in opposition to the other instincts, whose purpose is death. Somehow the formulation of the great opposition is concomitant with a confusion about the orientation of the sexual instincts. The opposition between Eros and Thanatos is usually taken as the point of reference to what the book is about. It functions as a landmark for readers who fear getting lost in this confusing text. Yet the very installation of this landmark seems to occasion a difficulty in ascertaining direction.

Perhaps we have ventured onto territory in which the very logic of opposition is one that cannot help but lead us astray. But at the same time without clear opposition, we feel lost; without polarity, we can have no compass. We are, seemingly, not far from the dilemma in which one can find Vienna only if things are not where they are supposed to be.

I can only hope, then, that my confusion is a sign I am near Vienna. When I drafted this chapter, I spent nearly an hour searching for a quotation in which Lacan says that the only way to advance is to return to Freud's texts. I wanted to use the quotation to point out the confusion about whether Lacan is advancing or returning. The quotation was not where I was absolutely sure it was. I became more and more distressed as I kept going back to look for it in the same place, unable to believe it was not there.

Returning to Freud's text, let us examine what happens to the instincts of self-preservation. Freud also calls these the ego-instincts, and in the terms of our analogy we are close here to that trend in psychoanalysis which wants to strengthen the ego, make it autonomous, and preserve it from outside incursions. In short, ego psychology seems to be serving the same ends as the instincts of self-preservation, self-assertion, and mastery. Prior to *Beyond the Pleasure Principle,* Freud divided the instincts into two groups: sexual and self-preservative (or ego-) instincts. But now it turns out that the sexual instincts "are the true life instincts." The place of the self-preservative instincts, which appear to be life instincts, becomes confused.[5]

> The instincts of self-preservation, of self-assertion and of mastery . . . are component instincts whose function it is to assure that the organism shall follow its own path to death, and to ward off any possible ways of returning to inorganic existence other than those which are immanent in the organism itself . . . . Thus these guardians of life, too, were originally the myrmidons of death. Hence arises the paradoxical situation that the living organism struggles most energetically against events (dangers, in fact) which might help it to attain its life's aim [that is, death] rapidly—by a kind of short-circuit. [P. 39]

If the death instinct aims to return to an earlier state, death must be the right kind of death, must be a repetition. The ego-instincts guard against any death but that which will be a return. They thus appear to serve life but actually serve death.

If we superimposed ego psychology on the place of the ego-instincts, we might say that ego psychology appears to be serving life, but it is actually serving death. That indeed is what Lacan suggests. For example, in "The Freudian Thing" he snidely says that his lectern would be the ideal patient for the ego psychologists (*E,* 425; *S,* 136), implying that although ego

5. For an excellent discussion of this realignment, see chapter 6 of Jean Laplanche, *Vie et mort en psychanalyse* (Paris: Flammarion, 1970). Translated by Jeffrey Mehlman as *Life and Death in Psychoanalysis* (Baltimore: Johns Hopkins University Press, 1976).

psychology appears to want to strengthen the ego, its real aim is an inanimate ego.

Freud has posited the reactionary nature of all instincts, but the self-preservative instincts do not appear to aim toward a return. The only way he can account for them is to see them working with (in fact, for) the death instincts. He then winds up with what he calls a "paradoxical situation": life is preserved so that the organism can "die only in its own fashion" (*S.E.* XVIII, 39).

At the end of this description of the paradoxical situation of the ego instincts, according to an editor's footnote, "in the editions before 1925 the following footnote appeared . . . 'A correction of this extreme view of the self-preservative instincts follows.'" Uncomfortable with the paradox, Freud first adds a footnote promising to attenuate its extremity. But later he removes the footnote, for no such correction, in any edition, follows. In fact, what does follow is a description not of the self-preservative instincts but of the sexual instincts, the description in which he says both that the sexual instincts restore an earlier state and that they do not.

Freud recognizes a paradox—concerning the ego-instincts—which he would like to correct. But in place of that correction is a contradiction that does not seem to disturb him. It is as if the contradictory nature of the sexual instincts is, in some way, the corrective for the paradoxical situation of the ego-instincts.[6]

In an effort to correct a disturbing situation, Freud repeats it—just as, in the beginning of *Beyond the Pleasure Principle*, the victims of traumas return to the traumatic scene in their dreams and the infant repeats the painful scene of his mother's departure. One might say that Freud acts out the mechanism he seeks to understand (the repetition compulsion) rather than explaining it.

Rather than resolving the problem of which side the ego-

6. In 1925, when Freud removes this footnote, he adds a note two pages earlier: "The reader should not overlook the fact that what follows is the development of an extreme line of thought. Later on, when account is taken of the sexual instincts, it will be found that the necessary limitations and corrections are applied to it" (p. 37).

instincts are on, life or death, Freud radicalizes the paradox. We are left with an opposition in which both terms have a contradictory orientation. We are thus left with a pure, formal opposition, without any orientation or aim. But how, then, can we determine which side is heading in the right direction?

Getting increasingly anxious, having become lost in the mires of Freud's text, I wonder how I will ever find my way back to Lacan. I am trying to ascertain the direction and the correctness of Lacan's "Return to Freud," but instead I find myself acting it out. My pretext for entering Freud's book was that it might illuminate the opposition between Lacan and ego psychology. However the complexity of Freud's text makes it increasingly difficult to contemplate actually using it to explain anything else.

How to get back? Where is the correct path? I keep returning to this question, and then, with the relief of recognition, it dawns on me that the primacy of this question is precisely Freud's discovery in *Beyond the Pleasure Principle*. The paradoxical situation which Freud never corrects is his discovery of a basic drive, so basic that it is beyond or before the opposition between death and self-preservation. That basic drive aims to "assure that the organism shall follow its own path to death." As Freud points out, the organism fights against the dangers that would hasten it to its goal, death. He considers this paradoxical and would like to rectify it but does not, and in that way he remains faithful in his rendering of a drive which he names the death instinct, but which, if we are to understand the collusion between it and the self-preservative instincts, we must understand as the drive to follow one's path to death. The goal of the drive is not its apparent endpoint, death, but "one's own path."

Freud also expresses this as "the organism wishes to die only in its own fashion." This formulation resembles something Lacan says of desire in "The Freudian Thing": "the desire for recognition dominates in its determinations the desire that is to be recognized, by conserving it as such until it be recognized" (*E*, 431; *S*, 141). Lacan sees in the sexual drives a primacy of recognition over the attainment of the goal desired. In order for the desire to be recognizable, it must pursue its aim "only in its own fashion." It is more important that a desire pursue the correct path—that is, its own path—to fulfillment than that it be fulfilled.

According to Lacan this primacy of recognition is "the necessary and sufficient condition" for "the repetitive insistence of [infantile] desires in the transference and their permanent recollection in a signifier where the repressed returns [*fait retour*]" (*E*, 431; *S*, 141). Thus Lacan explains two principal phenomena in psychoanalysis—the return of the repressed and transference—by the primacy of recognition. Both these phenomena are forms of repetition, types of returns. A desire must insistently repeat itself until it be recognized. If satisfaction, the reduction of tension, were the true goal of a desire, it might find a more efficient path than repeated insistence, just as, if the goal of the death instinct were simply the reduction of all tension, it could surely find a quick path to death. Thus repetition, that basic fact of psychoanalysis which Freud attempted to puzzle out in *Beyond the Pleasure Principle,* is the effect not so much of the frustration of a desire but of the lack of recognition of a desire. From this, we understand Lacan's notion of psychoanalysis as a context conducive to the subject's recognition of his desires.

The reader is likely to have recognized in the phrase for the return of the repressed the word "retour," with which Lacan describes his own enterprise. Is Lacan's return to Freud a return of the repressed? Shoshana Felman writes: "Since what returns in the Lacanian 'return' is, precisely, what is *unassimilable* in Freud, the return to Freud is not unlike the return of the repressed."[7] Felman's answer to our question is coy. The double negation ("not unlike") may be either *précieux* understatement or precise rendering of a complicated relation, and it may be both. In any case, the subtlety of her answer is in marked contrast to the lack of equivocation of Lacan's statement on the

7. Shoshana Felman, "The Originality of Jacques Lacan," *Poetics Today,* 2:1b (1980–81), 46; Felman's italics.

same issue. Speaking of his project of a "return to Freud" in "The Freudian Thing," he says: "It is not a question of a return of the repressed for us" (*E*, 403; *S*, 116).

Given a certain perverse reading, however, Lacan's unequivocal statement is no less ambiguous than Felman's. The negation seems gratuitous: he brings up the notion of the return of the repressed to no other purpose here than to deny its similarity to his return. Freud, in an article called "Negation," writes about just such gratuitous denegation: "We realize that this is a rejection, by projection, of an idea, that has just come up."[8] Suspicion about this unequivocal negation is further aggravated by study of the entire sentence in which it appears: "It is not a question of a return of the repressed for us, but of finding support in the antithesis constituted by the phase traversed by the psychoanalytic movement since the death of Freud, so as to demonstrate what psychoanalysis is not, and to seek with you the means to restore to power what never ceased to sustain it even in its deviation, that is, the primary meaning [*sens*] that Freud preserved there by his very presence."

The terms in this sentence once again recall the section we studied in *Beyond the Pleasure Principle*. There is an "antithesis" which in some ways opposes a death and a life, in this case Freud's. His life "preserves" something while his death brings on its antithesis. But the word "preserves" recalls the paradoxical situation of the self-preservative drives, which appear to be antithetical to death, but actually serve it. Might not the effect of Freud's living presence be likewise ambiguous? One might of course mention that the living Freud entrusted psychoanalysis to precisely those people whom Lacan considered antithetical to its "primary meaning," that Freud trusted people—like Marie Bonaparte and his daughter Anna—who in 1953 denied international affiliation to the group responsible for this "return to Freud."

Yet Lacan seems to consider that Freud's presence somehow magically preserved his meaning, his direction. Thus what Lac-

8. Sigmund Freud, "Negation," *S.E.* xix, 235.

an must "restore to power" is something akin to Freud's living presence. William Kerrigan, who, because he is not a Lacan specialist, sees certain things clearly, remarks that Lacan "wanted to recover nothing more and nothing less than the root of it: the living Freud . . . . Lacan's repeated claim to inhabit the living meaning of Sigmund Freud cannot be dismissed as readily as some suppose."[9]

It seems odd that Lacan should place such faith in the rule of the living father of psychoanalysis. Indeed, Freud tells a story about the rule of the living father, a story that supports what in Lacan's version of psychoanalysis will become the notion of the rule of the dead father, the symbolic father.

In *Totem and Taboo*, Freud recounts the story of how the sons banded together to kill the father so they could have the women the father kept to himself. But when the father was dead, they began to feel remorse. "The dead father became stronger then the living one had been . . . . What had up to then been prevented by his actual existence was thenceforward prohibited by the sons themselves . . . . They revoked their deed by forbidding the killing of the totem, the substitute for their father; and they renounced its fruits by resigning their claim to the women who had now been set free."[10]

Although at first he bases these two renunciations upon the psychological factor of remorse, Freud goes on to find another sort of factor behind the incest taboo. "Though the brothers had banded together in order to overcome their father, they were all one another's rivals in regard to the women. Each of them would have wished, like his father, to have all the women to himself. The new organization would have collapsed in a struggle of all against all . . . . Thus the brothers had no alternative, if they were to live together, but . . . to institute the law against incest . . . . In this way they rescued the organization which had made them strong" (*S.E.*, xiii, 144).

9. William Kerrigan, "Introduction," in Smith and Kerrigan, eds., *Interpreting Lacan*, p. x.

10. Sigmund Freud, *Totem and Taboo*, S.E. xiii, 143.

In order to transcend the unlivable rivalry of ego versus ego, in order to constitute a society, the sons had to take on the incest taboo, that is, they had to accept the rule of the dead father. The first structure, rivalry over objects, is what Lacan calls the imaginary order. The second, the truly social structure, he calls the symbolic. The symbolic is the rule of the dead father, "stronger than the living one." The subject must internalize the taboo on the father's women and, precisely because the father is already dead, give up the fantasy of overthrowing and replacing the father.

What then does it mean for Lacan to seek to "restore to power" the living father? It would seem that here we encounter Lacan's imaginary. That he would like to be a father of psychoanalysis as Freud was: "Wo Es war, soll Ich werden," Where Freud's presence, "the root," as Kerrigan calls it, "the Freudian Thing" was, I must come to be.

If through this passage from *Totem and Taboo* we see the transcendence of rivalry in the acceptance of the rule of the dead father, then we might associate Lacan's wish for the living father with his adversarial relation with the ego psychologists that runs through "The Freudian Thing." Kerrigan makes the same association: "He belonged . . . to the generation of psychoanalytic theorists who were able to imagine that Freud, a living presence for about half their lives, might really have been their father—and the French son was intensely aware of his position with respect to his imaginative siblings" (p. ix).

Lacan pulls no punches in his insults to American psychoanalysis. His basic criticism is that it never gets beyond "the language of the ego" (*E*, 429; *S*, 139)—a language in which there is nothing but the violent mutual exclusivity of rivalry. Lacan in his psychoanalysis would accede to the symbolic order, where it is not one ego talking to an alter, rival ego but rather a subject talking to a radical other, the Other. But in "The Freudian Thing," particularly in his attack on ego psychology, Lacan is himself mired in the imaginary, caught up in a rivalry over who is the true inheritor of Father Freud's psychoanalysis.

This does *not*, let us be clear, invalidate Lacan's text nor render it merely an example of pathology. His criticism of a psychoanalysis that is locked into imaginary discourse is well taken. But what remains to be seen is whether American psychoanalysis really is mired in the impasses of rivalry *and* whether his psychoanalysis is not. A Lacanian interpretation of ego psychology has yet to be performed,[11] if by "Lacanian" we mean not that which shares Lacan's own imaginary rivalry, the position of his ego, but a method of receiving discourse that fully assumes the death of the father, the impossibility of returning to Vienna.

If Vienna is the "eternal place" of the discovery that things are not where we expected, then not only is the location of Vienna unmappable but we cannot be sure Vienna is not in America. This disorienting psychoanalytic geography has left us with a pure antithesis in which both sides are engaged in "returns," but the direction of either becomes confused. There would be nothing for us but to be lost in the mirrors of the imaginary, except that, finally, there is another sort of "return" in "The Freudian Thing"—a return that is perhaps beyond the adversarial imaginary of the "return to Freud."

Lacan is criticizing the "orientation" of contemporary analysis for objectifying the subject. As a signal that, for our particuliar journey we are on the right track, we find here the word "sens" used for once in this text explicitly in the sense of "direction": "you cannot at the same time yourself proceed in this objectification of the subject and speak to him as you should . . . for the reason . . . that is expressed in the saying that one cannot serve two masters, that is, one cannot conform one's being to two actions that are oriented in opposite directions [*s'orientent en*

11. Joseph Smith, in his epilogue to *Interpreting Lacan*, gestures in the direction of a new encounter between Lacanian psychoanalysis and ego psychology, one beyond the binary oppositions of the imaginary order: "The particular conflict of interpretations here discussed has often been taken as presenting only a black-or-white choice: . . . ego psychology or . . . Lacan. I have shown . . . how the conflict could reach this degree of sharpness only by virtue of a careless or tendentious reading of both texts. A careful reading once again brings into view an area of compatibility ordinarily unrecognized by Lacanians and ego psychologists" (pp. 266–67).

sens contraire]" (*E*, 419; *S*, 130). Lacan then goes on to propose how analysis should operate if it would avoid the impasse of being oriented in two opposite directions:

> it is not about him [the analysand] that you have to speak to him . . . if it is to him that you have to speak, it is literally about something else . . . which is *the thing which is speaking to you, a thing* which . . . will always remain inaccessible to him, if, being speech which is addressed to you, it could not evoke in you its reply and if, having heard its message in this inverted form, you could not, by returning [*retourner*] it to him, give him the double satisfaction of having recognized it and making him recognize its truth. [*E*, 419–20; *S*, 130–31; italics mine]

The "return" that really counts in psychoanalysis is not the return to Freud but the return to the subject, and return is not an intransitive but a transitive verb. The analyst must return *something* to the subject. The analyst does not talk about the subject. Not only would that be objectification, but there is no way that the analyst could avoid giving her own imaginary projections, the language of her own ego. What the analyst must do is reply to what she hears. That reply sends back to the subject in inverted form (a reply being the inverse of the original statement) what he was saying (not from his ego but from elsewhere, from the thing, from *Es*) that he could never hear if he did not hear it returning from the analyst. Thus is accomplished the recognition that is the goal of analysis, recognition finally not by the other but by the subject. The subject must come to recognize his own drives, which are insisting, unbeknownst to him, in his discourse and his actions. That recognition is reached through the mediation of the analyst. The analyst returns to the subject what the subject was saying so that the subject can recognize it and stop saying it. That is the only return that matters in psychoanalysis, that is the analyst's only task.

What, then, if the return to Freud were really this kind of return—transitive? Not a return to Freud's presence but a return by Lacan to Freud's text of what Freud was saying that never got recognized. If, as Felman suggests, Lacan's return is a return of the repressed, but a return of the repressed in a psychoanalytic context where the repressed can be recognized and returned by the interlocutor to the subject for whom it was inaccessible, then it would be a truly psychoanalytic return to Freud. Lacan, by hearing the thing that spoke in Freud, by hearing the Freudian Thing, could recognize it and return it to Freud's text.

Only then, once the Freudian Thing were recognized, could Father Freud really be laid to rest. Only then could Father Freud, having found his own path, die.

Having completed this reading of "The Freudian Thing," there is more I want to say, but I cannot, now. I would like to say something about the dazzling style and force, about the extraordinary performance that is this text. I would like to talk about the two prosopopeia: one in which "truth speaks," the other in which Lacan lends his voice to his lectern. There is an incredible energy and passion that is somehow tied to the rivalry with American psychoanalysis. What I have called the imaginary dimension to Lacan's paper is not only its weak point; it is also its appeal, its beauty. But I am not yet able to deal with that. I feel some inhibition against touching the beautiful, crazy, violent portions of the text, some taboo against understanding how they work. I am not ready to understand what it means that beauty is so closely intricated with the imaginary. I might say that this is my resistance. Resistance, however, as Lacan defines it: "Resistance is the current state of an interpretation of the subject. It is the manner in which at that very moment, the subject interprets the point where he is . . . . It's you who call that resistance. It simply means that he cannot advance any faster, and you have nothing to say about that" (S, II, 266). Someday, perhaps, I'll be able to talk about the dramatic beauty of Lacan's imaginary.

September 10, 1981

Today, just a few days after drafting the preceding chapter, I learned Lacan had died.

INTERSTORY

Summer, 1982
On October 5, 1981, I began analysis. It was four days a week,
strict (American) Freudian psychoanalysis. I had decided about
six months earlier to do it, but in the interval I experienced
several periods of acutely anxious ambivalence, which generally
focused on time and money. Could I afford it? Before deciding
to begin, I had calculated that I could. There was a general
symptomatic forgetting of these calculations. And of course time
seemed incalculable. The time amounted to twelve hours a
week, since there was an hour drive to and from Cincinnati
involved. Could I get any work (writing) done while I was in
analysis? After all, I was in the middle of a book project.

On December 5, 1981, I quit my analysis. The decision affords
several interpretations. During the first month I had produced a
good number of hysterical, sexual symptoms, and experienced a
lot of fear and trembling: fear that analysis would make me
hysterical and literal trembling of the midsection of my body,
midriff, during a few sessions. During the second month the
fear and trembling subsided; my sexual life returned to "normal." One morning while I was reading Freud, I realized that
what I wanted from analysis was to understand everything enigmatic about me, what my dreams mean, why I was so afraid of

fishbones and of diving into water. I realized that when I read Freud (but not Lacan) I got the impression that all this could, someday, be understood. That, then, was what I wanted from analysis. This is, I believe, what Lacan means by the phallus. The phallus "designates as a whole the effects of signification" (*E*, 690; *S*, 285; *FS*, 80). If I had the phallus, then I would know what all my signifiers meant, I would command the play of signification. Freud writes in "Analysis Terminal and Interminable" that every woman ultimately wants a penis from her analyst, which is why analysis is interminable (*S.E.* XXIII, 252). If Lacan says that everyone is castrated, I understand that to mean not only do men no more have the phallus than women, but psychoanalysts have it no more than literature professors. These two for me were obviously linked, as I saw myself expressing various forms of psychoanalyst-envy in my analysis, resenting him, angrily, irrationally, and inconsolably, because he had so much more (money) than I. From reading Freud and Lacan, I had developed, already, a transference onto psychoanalysis in general. I believed psychoanalysis knew, and that if I were analyzed, or better yet if I became an analyst (my analysis was started under the guise of a training analysis), then I would get "it." I thought that Lacan considers the goal of analysis to be the analysand's assumption of his castration. To assume mine, it seemed to me, would mean understanding that I would never get transparent knowledge of myself from psychoanalysis or elsewhere, and thus never achieve (phallic) self-mastery. That whatever knowledge can be gained by psychoanalytic practice (no doubt considerable) is not more absolute, true, and phallic than whatever knowledge I enjoyed through reading, writing, and pedagogical practice. Suddenly it seemed no longer worth it to be in analysis, to spend so much time and money. I had gone into analysis, it seemed, because I felt unauthorized as a reader and writer of psychoanalytic theory, illegitimate because there was no practice behind my theory. Now I thought that assuming my castration meant assuming my inevitable illegitimacy, that I of course had a practice (reading and writing), and whatever practice one had was never enough. One never had the right to speak. I then decided that I had worked out the major reason for going into analysis, I had worked through my transference onto psychoanalysis in general, and now I would quit, no longer feeling anxiety about being or not being analyzed.

That afternoon I told this to my analyst. He agreed that it made sense but suggested that I wanted to quit because I had momentarily regained control and was afraid to lose it again. I was afraid of what analysis would unleash and uncover. I will not deny that fear. I felt that I was a chicken, quitting something out of fear. And so that day I did not quit. But at the next session I did. Although I felt depressed because I was a quitter. A few weeks later I was lunching with a friend, a Jungian analyst, telling her the story of my quitting analysis. She suggested that perhaps it was good for me for once to dare to quit, to admit failure.

When telling the analyst (mine) about quitting, I realized I wanted to write up an account of my brief encounter with analysis and put it into the book I was working on (actually the book I was not working on while I was in analysis). I finished Chapter 4 the month before beginning. I would write Chapter 5 the month after quitting. I wished to see the analysis as part of the process of writing the present book, of working through my transference onto Lacan. I was pleased at the idea of circumscribing my experience within my book. Also suspicious of that gesture. I wanted to write him (my analyst) into my scenario, to retain control.

May 25, 1984

Post-Script

As I finish off my manuscript, I am currently in therapy, have been for three months, with a woman psychologist who is neither a physician nor a psychoanalyst.

5

Metaphor and Metonymy

On May 9, 1957, Lacan delivered a lecture at the Sorbonne. This lecture, which appears in slightly revised form in *Ecrits*, is entitled "L'Instance de la lettre dans l'inconscient ou la raison depuis Freud" (The Agency of the Letter in the Unconscious or Reason since Freud). Jean-Luc Nancy and Philippe Lacoue-La-barthe, in their reading of this text, mention that it is "the first real intervention by Lacan in the University."[1] The capital "U" in their comment reminds us that the Sorbonne is, in France, *the* University, that it is, in some way, the very symbol of the academic institution at its most traditional. Lacan is thus intervening in the reigning order of knowledge, not simply in the university as a place but in the University as a symbolic structure. This same text also becomes (perhaps not coincidentally) Lacan's "first real intervention" in the American academy. Appearing in 1966 in the *Yale French Studies* issue on structuralism (under the title "The Insistence of the Letter in the Unconscious"), it is the first of the *Ecrits* to be translated into English.

It is worth noting that the lecture was given at the request of the Philosophy Group of the Fédération des Étudiants ès Let-

1. Nancy and Lacoue-Labarthe, *Le Titre de la lettre*, p. 19. Henceforth referred to as "Titre."

tres. "Etudiants ès Lettres" corresponds roughly to what we could call "Students in the Humanities." However, let us not translate too quickly this phrase that Sheridan leaves in the original French. In this context "Humanities" and "Letters" have quite different associations. Whereas Lacan ends his lecture by pointing to "humanistic man" as the "object" of our "indignation" (E, 528; S, 175), throughout the lecture he is promulgating the power of the "letter" and establishing something Nancy and Lacoue-Labarthe call the "science of the letter." The phrase "Students in the Humanities" translates the spirit of "Etudiants ès Lettres" but not the letter. Yet the difference between the spirit and the letter, the question of the preeminence of one over the other, may be precisely what is at stake in the difference between "Humanities" and "Letters."

Lacan, at the beginning of the lecture, poses the question of how to take the "letter" in his title. He answers, "quite simply, à la lettre" (E, 405; S, 147). A la lettre: that is, literally, "to the letter"; figuratively, "literally." Sheridan translates with "literally," but adds a footnote that supplies the French. This problem of a translation of "à la lettre," of a translation à la lettre, marks with an efflorescence of bad jokes the point where a conflict between the spirit and the letter becomes telling.

The very first page of Lacan's Ecrits begins with the Buffon quote "Le style est l'homme même," another locution that is difficult to translate. I would render it with something like "Style is [the] man himself [or itself]" or "Style is the essence of [the] man" or "Style makes the man." I can probably convey the spirit, but what gets lost in my translation is precisely the style.

In a first approximation I might line up the object of study of the Humanities with l'homme, whereas the object of study of Letters would be le style. Lacan's monumental book begins with what would seem to be the very assertion of identity between style and man. However, the balance between the two is upset precisely by that which literally appears on the side of l'homme, but which as we try to translate seems to have more to do with style; that is, the balance is upset by the word "même." That word is identity itself (l'identité même), capable of expressing both identity with something else and self-identity. Yet "même," there to underline the identity between the object of the Humanities and the object of the Letters, in this case impedes smooth translation, causes a disjunction between spirit and letter to appear.

The disjunction which translation imposes upon us is not immediately available in French. Buffon and his statement are "classics": nothing here that could constitute a disruptive intervention in the Sorbonne. But Lacan goes on to produce his own version of Buffon's formula: "Style is the man to whom one addressess oneself" (Le style c'est l'homme à qui l'on s'adresse"). In the place of the "même," the translation's stumbling block, we find the interlocutor. The substitution of the interlocutor for the "même"—for the identical, for identity or self—is highly resonant with Lacan's notion of the ego as constituted through an identification with the other. We could here recall "The Mirror Stage." In the context of the present chapter, however, let us note that Lacan addresses himself to the Fédération des étudiants ès lettres.

Lacan has found his principal American audience among literary academics, and so this text addressed to those in Letters rather than to psychoanalysts is particularly appropriate for American readers of Lacan. Possibly this text was the first to be translated for that reason. I recently taught a seminar on psychoanalysis and literature for students of literature and chose "The Agency of the Letter" as the sole Lacan text in the syllabus. The aptness of this text for students ès lettres is not that it aids us in applying psychoanalysis to literature, nor even that it talks about literature proper at all. It has fewer literary allusions than many of Lacan's works. In his address to the students ès lettres, Lacan asserts that "Freud constantly maintained . . . [literary] training as the prime requisite for the formation of analysts, and . . . he designated the eternal universitas litterarum as the ideal place for its institution" (E, 494; S, 147). Rather than teach psychoanalysis as a basis for understanding literature, "The Agency of the Letter" implies that psychoanalysis itself be a regional branch of literary studies.

The object of psychoanalytic knowledge is traditionally considered to be man (object of the Humanities): psychoanalysis is a
branch of psychology. Through his emphasis on the intersubjective dialogue of the analytic experience as well as his discovery
that the ego itself is constituted in an intersubjective relation,
Lacan has shifted the object of psychoanalysis from the individual person taken as separate monad to the intersubjective
dialectic. One might now say that the object of psychoanalysis,
what it as science and practice seeks to discern, is "the man to
whom one addresses oneself." In other words, words from the
second chapter of the present book, "the man to whom one
addresses oneself" is the imago projected onto the neutral
screen of the analyst. But as we read on the first page of *Ecrits*
"the man to whom one addresses oneself" is "style." The imago
is carried in the style of address. The object of psychoanalytic
study reveals itself as "style."

One might expect literary students to be at home in understanding Lacan. They have an apprenticeship in "style," have
learned how to appreciate it, how to analyze it, and, in the best
of cases, how to produce it. Yet my students had tremendous
difficulty reading "The Agency of the Letter." (Admittedly, this
was no surprise.) They came to class frustrated, disgruntled,
feeling inadequate or outraged. Despite all their literary training, the major obstacle was precisely Lacan's style.

Now, if Lacan's style is the major obstacle to reading Lacan,
and if style for Lacan is the interlocutor, then perhaps the block
to reading Lacan is the reader herself. Or rather, since Lacan
cannot address himself to the real reader but only to an imagined reader, perhaps the great difficulty in reading Lacan, the
great *malaise* produced by his style, resides in the discrepancy
the reader feels between her-self and the text's interlocutor,
whose place she occupies but does not fill. The violence of Lacan's style is its capacity to make the reader feel nonidentical with
herself as reader, or, in other more psychological terms, to make
the reader feel inadequate to her role as "the man to whom
Lacan addresses himself," that is, inadequate to Lacan's style.

In an attempt to induce the students to participate in reading

Lacan, I began class by attempting to delineate some of the features of his style. One of these is the peculiar quality of his paragraphing. Lacan's paragraphs tend to be brief and choppy. A great number of them consist of only one sentence. Some of these sentences are actually sentence fragments. Conventionally, a paragraph has unity and there is continuity between the sentences within it. In Lacan's prose the sentences tend towards isolation and discontinuity. For this reason, rather than flowing discursivity, rather than a continuous progression of ideas, we find a series of discontinuous elements.

Lacan reminds us that Freud compares the dream to a rebus.[2] A rebus is a picture-puzzle in which the elements do not belong together, have no representational unity. The only way to understand a rebus, to interpret it, is to consider the elements one at a time. Thus Freud formulates a basic rule of dream interpretation: one must separate each element for consideration. As we saw in Chapter 1, Muller and Richardson call Lacan's writings a rebus.[3] Lacan's text in its discontinuity seems to break apart into distinct elements. One cannot follow the argument, but if the reader is willing to concentrate on one sentence or fragment at a time, much can be understood. It is our habit of discursive reading, our assumption that each sentence flows out of the preceding one that undoes us in the face of Lacan's rebuslike text. When we consider one sentence at a time, many sentences make sense and some do not but, just as with a dream, an interpretation can be quite valuable even though some elements remain mysterious.

Having established the principle that the text could be approached like a dream, that we could interpret one element at a time rather than feel responsible for understanding the totality, I suggested that we turn to one of the most enigmatic and frustrating parts of the text—the "algorithms" for metonymy and metaphor—and try our hand at interpreting them. These for-

2. *Ecrits*, p. 510; *Ecrits: A Selection*, p. 159. Freud says this in *The Interpretation of Dreams*, S.E. IV, 277–78.

3. Muller and Richardson, *Lacan and Language*, p. 3.

mulas are particularly intimidating to the literary student (Lacan's addressee). The assumption is that there is some logico-mathematical operation here that the reader cannot understand. But in fact these algorithms are absurd. As Nancy and Lacoue-Labarthe remark, these formulas "cannot in fact be read as real logical formulas (they neither suppose nor authorize, here, any calculation)" (*Titre*, 99). This realization releases us literary types from the obligation to master the operations and allows us to read.

An entire section of Chapter VI of Freud's *Interpretation of Dreams* is devoted to calculations in dreams. Freud writes there that "we may safely say that the dream-work does not in fact carry out any calculations at all, whether correctly or incorrectly; it merely throws into the *form* of a calculation numbers which are present in the dream-thoughts and can serve as allusions to matter that cannot be represented in any other way."[4] In Lacan's case the calculations consist of letters and not numbers, which not only heightens Lacan's insistence on the letter, but beckons a reading from the *étudiants ès lettres*.

Although they tend to dismiss the algorithms as a joke, Lacoue-Labarthe and Nancy do interpret one element of them in a footnote. The formula for metaphor contains an addition sign: +. Lacan writes of this: "the + sign . . . here manifesting the crossing of the bar" (*E*, 515; *S*, 164). The "bar" is always represented in Lacan's notations as a horizontal line; it is therefore "crossed" by the vertical line in the + sign. In their footnote, Nancy and Lacoue-Labarthe note that the "ideographic skewing" of the "usual symbol of addition . . . has all the airs of a *Witz* on the logico-mathematical notation" (*Titre*, 100n). Lacan treats the addition sign as an ideogram; such treatment is a *Witz*, a joke, a visual pun. The pun is more blatant in the English translation where "franchissement de la barre" is rendered by "*crossing* of the bar." "Witz" is an allusion to the German title of *Jokes and Their Relation to the Unconscious*, in which Freud propounds the idea that the mechanisms of jokes are the same as

4. Freud, *The Interpretation of Dreams*, S.E. V, 418.

the mechanisms of dreams. The visual pun on the addition sign as a cross is a familiar mechanism of the rebus.

Lacoue-Labarthe and Nancy present no further deciphering of this rebus. Thanks to the obviousness of the pun in English, their reading of the + sign corresponds to what was the point of departure for me and my class. For the remainder of this chapter I will present my associations with the various elements in the two algorithms. In the spirit of a Freudian dream-interpretation, I will give not the "meaning" of the algorithms, but the necessarily contradictory and errant process of reading the following formulas:

METONYMY $\quad f(S. . .S')S \cong S(-)s$

METAPHOR $\quad f\left(\dfrac{S'}{S}\right) S \cong S(+)s$

$$[E, 515; S, 164]$$

Both of these are based on an earlier algorithm, one which, according to Lacan, founds modern linguistics: S/s. Although Lacan attributes this formula to Saussure, it differs in several significant ways from any of Saussure's formulations,[5] and so is actually, in letter if not in spirit, Lacan's creation. Lacan states that it should be read as "the signifier over the signified, 'over' corresponding to the bar separating the two stages" (E, 497; S, 149). At first this seems a "straight" formula, but even here there is an ideographic dimension. The signifier (S) is *over* the signified (s). Lacan will talk about the sovereignty or the rule of the signifier over signification. If "over correspond[s] to the bar [barre]," we might want to recall the French idiomatic expression "avoir barre sur" (literally, to have bar over), meaning to have the advantage over. The signifier is capital, and it is on top.

Lacoue-Labarthe and Nancy point out that in Saussure's formulations the signified is always on top (*Titre*, 38–39). Lacan's revision of Saussure is to put the signifier on top—that is, I would say, to give it preeminence. We could say that the sig-

5. See *Titre*, pp. 38–40.

nifier is the letter, the signified the spirit, and Lacan's gesture gives *instance* (that is—in a criticized neologistic but commonly used meaning—authority) to the letter.

In a psychoanalytic context, the notion of an above and a below can also remind us of depth psychology. The signified is here repressed into the depths of the unconscious. Its letter is not only small but in italic, as if it were more removed, foreign perhaps, from another realm.

And speaking of the letter, there is *the* letter, the only actual letter in the algorithms. The proliferation of S's creates a certain "insistence of the letter" (title of the *Yale French Studies* translation). The S insists and in its insistence, recalls the German *Es*, name of the id. (In *La Chose freudienne*, Lacan points out the homonymy between "Es" and "the initial letter of the word 'subject' "—*E*, 417; *S*, 129; see my preceding chapter). Finally, not unworthy of notice is the homonym "ès," that strange, archaic word retained only in academic usage. The phrase "ès lettres" might then be read S-letters, a description of our algorithms. Transferentially, I might add that my choice of *E* to refer to *Ecrits* and *S* to refer to Sheridan's translation produces an *ES* in my text whenever I quote Lacan. Postscripturally, I must add that as I was doing the final revisions on this chapter the S on my typewriter suddenly stopped working.

"*f*" represents function. The metaphoric function (S'/S) is simple to understand. Lacan defines metaphor as "one word for another" (*E*, 507; *S*, 158). The replaced word (old signifier) becomes the signified of the new word (signifier). But the metonymic function ($S \ldots S'$) is more difficult to grasp. It is more allusive, more—dare I say?—elliptical. Lacan defines metonymy as the relation word by word (*mot à mot*—*E*, 506; *S*, 156), which Roman Jakobson calls the relation of contiguity. It is the relation between two signifiers along the line of any concrete discourse (linear because only one word is pronounced or written at a time). For example, it can be the relation between two words in the same sentence or paragraph. In the metonymic dimension, the signifier can receive its complete signification only *après-coup* (by deferred action, after the fact).

I associate the ellipsis between S and S′ with the following paragraph, which appears earlier in the text: "For the signifier by its nature always anticipates meaning by unfolding in some way its dimension before it. As is seen at the level of the sentence when it is interrupted before the significative term: 'I shall never . . .', 'All the same it is . . .', 'And yet there may be . . .'. Such sentences are not without meaning, a meaning all the more oppressive in that it is content to make us wait for it" (*E*, 502; *S*, 153). For the moment, let us just note that the ellipsis, and therefore, perhaps, metonymy, is considered "oppressive."

One might say that the signifier for the metaphoric function in these algorithms itself functions as a metaphor and thus is easy to explain, since explanation demands only that we supply the old, replaced signifier (S/s has been replaced by S′/S). Likewise one could say that the signifier for the metonymic function (S . . . S′) is itself a metonymy and therefore demands an entire context to be understood. More ideograms.

Each algorithm contains two parentheses, one on either side of the congruence sign ($\cong$). (As to what "congruence" means here, I haven't a clue.) In the metonymy formula we find a minus sign—that is, a horizontal "bar"—on the right and a horizontal configuration of S and S′ on the left. The left parenthesis of the second formula is a vertical configuration of S and S′. The terms "horizontal" and "vertical" actually appear in the sentence introducing the two formulas: "horizontal signifying chain" and "vertical dependencies." The distinction between horizontal and vertical in language corresponds to Lacan's use of Jakobson's alignment of metonymy with the horizontal dimension of language (the line of Western writing, the syntagmatic) and metaphor with the vertical dimension (the paradigmatic stack of possible selections for any point along the line).

Lacoue-Labarthe and Nancy consider that the opposition between horizontal and vertical is not value-free in Lacan's text, but that horizontality is linked to insufficiency. They cite the following passage from "The Agency of the Letter": "But the linearity that F. de Saussure holds as constitutive of the chain of discourse, in conformity with its emission by a single voice and

with its *horizontal* inscription in our writing, if it is in fact necessary, *is not sufficient*" (*E*, 503; *S*, 154; emphasis mine). This sentence would not in itself constitute a link between horizontality
and insufficiency, but they find the the idea of sufficiency insists
since the next paragraph begins: "But *it suffices* [*il suffit*] to listen
to poetry . . . for a polyphony to be heard, for it to become clear
that all discourse is aligned along the several staves of a score"
(*Titre*'s emphasis). The horizontal is insufficient; the nonlinear
musical score (several staves) presents a sufficiency. Nancy and
Lacoue-Labarthe then comment: "As much as linearity causes
problems, so verticality (promised land . . .) goes without saying. And it is no coincidence if the latter is introduced here by a
metaphor—and by a metaphor (the analogy of music) that is
perhaps the metaphor of metaphor" (*Titre*, 58). The musical
score is nonlinear—that is, both horizontal and vertical—but
Nancy and Lacoue-Labarthe seem to think that Lacan is not
simply asserting the insufficiency of linearity, of any one dimension. The ironic parenthesis "(promised land . . .)" suggests
that for Lacan verticality promises sufficiency, wholeness, abun-
dance. The remark "it is no coincidence" implies that the val-
orizing of verticality is complicitous with a privileging of metaphor over metonymy.

Although the authors of *Titre* seem to confuse verticality and
nonlinearity in their interpretation of the image of the musical
score, a similar confusion can be seen at work in the algorithm
for metaphor. As I mentioned above, Lacan uses "horizontal"
and "vertical" in his introduction to the algorithms, suggesting
that one is horizontal and the other vertical. And in the metonymy formula, a horizontal configuration of S and S' is paired
with a horizontal line (the bar, the minus sign). But in the algorithm for metaphor, a vertical disposition of S and S' is
paired, not with a vertical line, but with a cross composed of a
vertical and a horizontal line. The setup of the algorithms encourages the reader to see only the vertical line, which "crosses
the bar," as representing metaphor. But what is actually in the
right hand parenthesis is not the vertical crossing line, but the
cross itself, two dimensional, nonlinear.

The text seems to supply two contradictory readings, a first, easier one that privileges the vertical, and another that shows that the privilege of the vertical is actually a confusion of the vertical with a nonlinear configuration that is both vertical and horizontal. And if the privilege of the vertical is wedded to the preference for metaphor, then a recognition of the two dimensions of the + suggests that metonymy is necessary for metaphor. Exactly one year before the lecture to the *étudiants ès lettres*, in his seminar of May 9, 1956, Lacan insists that "metonymy is there from the beginning, and it is what makes metaphor possible."[6]

Although our starting point in reading these algorithms was metaphor's cross as ideogram, the neat polarity of horizontal versus vertical made it very easy and gratifying to be taken in by metaphor's supposed verticality. Lacoue-Labarthe and Nancy's reading of metaphor's vertical promise is most tempting, and we will pursue this reading, the most obvious one, as a misreading invited by the text, all the while trying to remember that something else is also going on.

In the sentence following the metonymy algorithm, there are two occurrences of the words "manque" (lack). "Lack" has affinities to the minus sign of the right-hand parenthesis in the formula for metonymy as well as to the ellipsis of the left (S . . . S'). Where there is an ellipsis, something is missing. If the difference between metaphor and metonymy is that between a plus and a minus sign, between a more and a less, then metonymy bodies forth some lack. This lack, this minus might correspond to the "insufficiency" of horizontality.

In a psychoanalytic context, this binary opposition between a plus and a minus, between a lack and a nonlack, has resonances with sexual difference, or more specifically with a certain binary misreading of sexual difference, the opposition phallic/castrated. This opposition characterizes what Freud calls the

6. Lacan, *Le Seminaire* iii: *Les psychoses* (Paris: Seuil, 1981), p. 259. Henceforth referred to as *S* iii.

phallic phase, the last phase of infantile sexuality.[7] If we associate metonymy's horizontal insufficiency with this phallic lack, then the misreading of vertical privilege can be seen as the insistence of phallic phase reasoning, which is incorrect yet powerfully difficult to avoid.

In the sentence following the metaphor formula, Lacan says that in this vertical substitution "is produced an effect of signification which is that of poetry or of creation." Metonymy, that sad structure, horizontally laid out, offers up only lack; but metaphor reaches the heights of poetry or creation. Earlier in his lecture, Lacan talks about "the creative spark of metaphor" (E, 507; S, 157). A page later the expression "poetic spark" is found in close proximity with "paternal mystery." This word "creation," linked to metaphor and poetry, is not without its sexual, reproductive connotations. Yet once one is talking about reproduction, one is, supposedly, beyond the phallic phase and into adult sexuality.

In a footnote, Lacan comments on the algorithms: "S' designating . . . the term productive of the signifying effect . . . one can see that this term is latent in metonymy, patent in metaphor" (E, 515n; S, 178n.29). Whereas in metonymy S is separated from S' by an ellipsis (S' is latent, it is only anticipatory), in metaphor S' is on top (patent, if we remember the vertical resonance with depth psychology, the upper term is on the surface). If S' designates the "term productive of the signifying effect" and if that effect is somehow linked to sexual creation, then we might associate a "latent" S' with the internal, "hidden" female genitalia, whereas the male genitalia are "patent."[8]

For us "Students in the Letters," another association is tempting. Jakobson links metaphor to poetry (particularly to romantic

7. See Freud, "The Infantile Genital Organization," S.E. xix.

8. In "Some Psychical Consequences of the Anatomical Distinction between the Sexes," Freud, in explaining the castration complex in girls (penis envy), calls the penis "strikingly visible" (S.E. xix, 252). In the phallic phase, according to Freud, the female genitals are unknown, "latent" (S.E. xix, 142).

and symbolist poetry) and metonymy to the realist novel.[9] Lacan, as we have seen, explicitly links metaphor to poetry and also makes allusion to metonymy's tie to realism ("all 'realism' in creative work takes its virtue from metonymy"—*E*, 517–18; *S*, 166). The examples of realist metonymy Jakobson gives are both from Tolstoy: Anna Karenina's handbag and the synechdochic depiction of female characters in *War and Peace*. Lacan's seminar on May 9, 1956, devoted to metaphor and metonymy, likewise refers to Tolstoy in order to exemplify metonymy. "Metonymy is . . . appreciable in certain passages of Tolstoy's work; where each time it is a matter of the approach of a woman, you see emerging in her place, in a grand-style metonymic process, the shadow of a beauty mark, a spot on the upper lip, etc." (*S* III, 266). Lacan then goes on explicitly to link realism and metonymy: "In a general manner, metonymy animates this style of creation which we call, in opposition to symbolic style and poetic language, the so-called realist style." In both Jakobson and Lacan, a shadow of femininity haunts the juncture of metonymy and realism. It is not that either of them defines realism or metonymy as feminine (that would be a metaphoric, symbolic gesture), but that by contiguity, by metonymy, a certain femininity is suggested.

At the end of his article on the two types of aphasia, Jakobson complains that "nothing comparable to the rich literature on metaphor can be cited for the theory of metonymy" (p. 258). In his seminar of May 9, 1956, Lacan likewise finds a prejudice operating in favor of metaphor, and at the expense of metonymy: "the eternal temptation . . . is to consider that what is most apparent in a phenomenon is what explains everything. . . . linguists have been victims of this illusion. The accent they place for example on metaphor, always given much more study than metonymy, bears witness to it. . . . it is certainly what is most captivating" (*S* III, 255). Metaphor is more apparent than metonymy, and so it has been given greater consideration. But

9. Roman Jakobson, "Two Aspects of Language and Two Types of Aphasic Disturbances," in *Selected Writings*, II (Hague: Mouton, 1971), pp. 255–56.

its importance participates in an illusion, a "captivating" illusion. Something that might belong to Lacan's imaginary order, the order of captivating illusions, beginning with the mirror image. More apparent or, as Lacan says in commentary on the algorithms, "patent." Metaphor is patent; metonymy is latent. The latency, the hiddenness of metonymy, like that of the female genitalia, lends it an appearance of naturalness or passivity so that "realism"—"which we call . . . the so-called realist style," (S iii, 260)—appears either as the lack of tropes, or as somehow mysterious, the "dark continent" of rhetoric.[10]

Luce Irigaray, the feminist psychoanalyst who has taken most articulate and interesting exception to the phallocentrism of psychoanalytic theory, also "accuses the privilege of metaphor (quasi solid) over metonymy (which has much more to do with fluids)."[11] This accusation is made in an article called "The 'Mechanics' of Fluids," in which she complains that science has studied solids and neglected fluids. She then links this to the neglect of feminine sexuality in psychoanalysis, by means of assertions that the feminine is fluid. Whatever doubts one might have about her assertion of feminine fluidity, it is interesting to note that Irigaray connects the privilege of metaphor over metonymy with the phallocentric neglect of femininity.

Irigaray's article is a critique of Lacan, whom she accuses of neglecting fluids, and thus women, in favor of the solidity of the phallus. She does not explicitly say that he privileges metaphor over metonymy, but Nancy and Lacoue-Labarthe do. As we have seen, their accusation of prejudice against metonymy is accompanied by a misreading of two dimensions in the musical score as simple verticality. That misreading is another example of what, in 1956, Lacan calls the "eternal temptation to consider that what is most apparent in a phenomenon is what explains

10. "Dark continent" is a term Freud used for female sexuality, a term frequently quoted in French psychoanalytic works ("continent noir"). I have not yet succeeded in locating this term in Freud's text, but that may be my blind spot.

11. Luce Irigaray, "La 'Mécanique' des fluides" in *Ce Sexe qui n'en est pas un*, p. 108. For a discussion of this article in relation to Lacan see chap. 3 of Gallop, *The Daughter's Seduction*.

everything." Metaphor's vertical privilege is "what is most apparent" in "The Agency of the Letter." Lacan sees that "eternal temptation" as responsible for linguists' prejudice in favor of metaphor. But it is equally involved in our reading of Lacan's prejudice in favor of metaphor. As if, whatever side one were on, this temptation was intimately tied to the privilege of metaphor.

Lacan's preference for metaphor and verticality may be an "illusion," but it is one to which we all fall "victim." It is an "eternal temptation," which is to say, we cannot ever be safe from its lures. If this temptation, with its "captivating" illusions, belongs to the imaginary order, then we cannot get beyond it by refusing it but must, as I suggested in Chapter 2 above, fall for and contemplate these illusions so as to get at what is structuring them.

The most extreme and explicit form of metaphor's privilege in Lacan's text inhabits its association with liberation, which contrasts with metonymy's link to servitude. As we noted above, metonymy's ellipsis can be considered "oppressive" (E, 502; S, 153). Metaphor, on the other hand, is "the crossing of the bar." The word for "crossing"—"franchissement"—has an older meaning of liberation from slavery, enfranchisement. The "bar" is an obstacle; metaphor unblocks us. Let us recall the association between the bar and repression mentioned briefly above. Michèle Montrelay, a Lacanian analyst, writes that the analyst's discourse is "a *metaphor* of the patient's discourse."[12] The analyst's intervention frees the patient from his suffering by allowing him to metaphorize.

In a passage that occurs some pages before the algorithms, "metaphor" again appears in proximity to "franchi" (crossed, but also enfranchised). Then, in the next paragraph, the question is posed as to whether metonymy "does not manifest some servitude inherent in its presentation" (E, 508; S, 158). This

---

12. Michèle Montrelay, "Inquiry into Femininity," trans. Parveen Adams, *m/f* 1 (1978), 86; her emphasis. Originally published as "Recherches sur la fémininité," *Critique* 278 (1970), 670.

paragraph where we find "metonymy" and "servitude" also includes "obstacle," "social censorship," and "oppression." My reading of links such as that between "metaphor" and "franchi" when they occur in the same sentence or between "metonymy" and other words in the same paragraph might be called a metonymic reading. Whereas a metaphoric interpretation would consist in supplying another signifier which the signifier in the text stands for (a means b; the tie represents a phallus), a metonymic interpretation supplies a whole context of associations. Perhaps this metonymic interpretation might be called feminine reading.

Metonymy is servitude; the subject bows under the oppressive weight of the bar. Metaphor is a liberation from that weight. Yet, as Nancy and Lacoue-Labarthe remind us, metaphor "must borrow the tricks and detours" of metonymy "in order to produce itself" (*Titre*, 58). Feminine metonymy has tricks and detours that, according to Lacan, allow it to "get around the obstacles of social censorship" (*E*, 508; *S*, 158). Masculine metaphor may be frank (*franc, franchi*), may be free of the obstacles shackling femininity, but it is dependent on feminine metonymy to "[re]produce itself." As Lacan puts it a year earlier in his seminar, "Metonymy is there from the beginning, and it is what makes metaphor possible" (*S* III, 259). The linearity of language may not be "sufficient," but it is "necessary" (*E*, 503; *S*, 154—see discussion above). The phallic phase model of thinking (binary opposition between phallus and lack, vertical and horizontal) can applaud metaphor's freedom and demean metonymy's servitude. But the adult sexual model sees the masculine dependency on the feminine, sees the horizontal bar in metaphor's cross.

Something like a reading of Lacan's phallocentrism has begun to manifest itself in this study of the privilege of metaphor.[13]

13. Lacoue-Labarthe and Nancy come close to such a critique in one footnote. But they end the footnote by saying "It would thus remain—but this surpasses our intentions here—to tie all this to the motif that seems to dominate . . . a text like 'The Signification of the Phallus'" (*Titre*, 95n).

Nonetheless, such a reading necessitates attention to the signification of the phallus in Lacan's work. "The Signification of the Phallus" is, of course, the title of another essay in *Ecrits*, the subject, in fact, of my next chapter. But I find a certain anticipation unavoidable.

Anticipation seems more and more to be the key notion for my reading of Lacan—one that returns, although differently, in every chapter. In "The Agency of the Letter," "anticipation" occurs in the context of incomplete sentences, in the paragraph we associated with the metonymic ellipsis. This anticipation, Lacan tells us, can be "seen . . . when [the sentence] is interrupted before the significative term" (*E*, 502; *S*, 153). The term "phallus" never appears in "The Agency of the Letter." I find myself compelled to read this text as if it were one of those sentences "interrupted before the significative term," and so this chapter will anticipate the Signification of the Phallus.

In that essay we find the assertion that the phallus "can play its role only when veiled" (*E*, 692: *S*, 288; *FS*, 82). This veiled phallus has associations with Freud's notion of the maternal phallus (phallic mother), to which Lacan explicitly refers (*E*, 686; *S* 282; *FS*, 76). Returning to our algorithms where Lacan designates the significative term by S', we could here consider S' as designating the phallus ("latent" in metonymy/mother, "patent" in metaphor/father). This reading ultimately suggests that metonymy is more truly phallic than metaphor and that it is in "The Agency of the Letter," rather than in "The Signification of the Phallus," that the phallus plays its role.

Lacan's complete sentence from "The Signification of the Phallus" reads: "All these propositions do nothing yet but veil [*voiler*] the fact that it can play its role only when veiled [*voilé*], that is to say, as itself a sign of the *latency* with which every signifiable is struck, as soon as it is raised to the function of the signifier" (my italics). This mention of "latency" recalls metonymy, and it turns out there is an even more insistent link between this passage with its two "veils" and metonymy. In "The Agency," Lacan's example of metonymy is: thirty sails [*voiles*] for thirty ships. Lacan comments that the malaise created by this classic example "veiled [*voilait*] less these illustrious sails [*voiles*] than the definition they were supposed to illustrate" (*E*, 505; *S*, 156). The "voile" in "Agency" (sail) is feminine, whereas "voile" meaning "veil" is masculine. But "voile" for "sail" is derived from "voile" for "veil," and it may be just this sort of slippage between a masculine and a feminine term that is at play in Lacan's notion of the phallus, which is a latent phallus, a metonymic, maternal, feminine phallus.

If metonymy in "Agency" thus anticipates the phallus in the later text, then, retrospectively, our earlier association of metonymy with lack and metaphor with phallus becomes problematic. Of course, both readings must be taken into account. Our first reading, which replaces metonymy by castration, must be here termed a metaphoric reading in that, by use of similarity (Jakobson's metaphoric relation), it replaces one term by another. Our second reading, the one which anticipates the latent context of "The Signification of the Phallus," would be more properly a metonymic reading of metonymy.

A metonymic reading construes metonymy as phallic whereas a metaphoric interpretation attributes the phallus to metaphor. Either sort of reading inevitably locates the phallus in its own narcissistic reflection in the text. What we may be approaching here is some sort of pathology of interpretation, and as I struggle with this portion of my reading/writing, struggle with my own narcissistic investment in my own phallus (femininely latent of course), a nausea, a paralysis creeps over me, a difficulty in going further, an aphasia on the level of metalanguage.

In Jakobson's article on the two types of aphasic disturbances, we read (p. 248) that the "loss of metalanguage" is characteristic of "similarity disorder." "Similarity disorder" means a speaker can operate quite well in the metonymic dimension, but experiences a breakdown in the metaphoric dimension. As I have progressively moved into and privileged a metonymic reading, I have suffered greater and greater difficulty in maintaining metalanguage.

Jakobson, as I mentioned earlier, points out a tendency in literary scholarship to privilege metaphor. His article concludes with the following statement (pointing toward a pathology of interpretation): "The actual bipolarity has been artificially replaced in these studies by an amputated, unipolar schema which, strikingly enough, coincides with one of the two aphasic patterns, namely with the contiguity disorder" (p. 259). Our mistaking the metaphoric formula as vertical (unipolar) rather than vertical *and* horizontal (bipolar) might be an example of the interpretive pathology Jakobson diagnoses. A unipolar schema in place of a bipolar one resembles the thinking characteristic of Freud's phallic phase. In the phallic phase, only one kind of genital organ comes into account—the male; the real female genitals are unknown.[14]

I have suggested links between what Jakobson calls the traditional "amputated, unipolar schema" and phallocentrism. Celebrating a new, feminine metonymic reading (which, as opposed to the metaphoric, I have *not* called interpretation), I have sought to go beyond that phallocentric interpretive tradition. But my metonymic reading has led me to the notion of the latent phallus, and I have come to see that, in its own way, metonymic interpretation can be phallocentric too. I realize that it would be yielding to simply another "amputated, unipolar schema" to choose the metonymic dimension and neglect the metaphoric. Any polar opposition between metaphor and metonymy (vertical versus horizontal, masculine versus feminine) is trapped in the imaginary order, subject to the play of identification and rivalry. One antidote to the "eternal temptation" to privilege metaphor might be, however, to recognize the horizontal line in metaphor's cross, the bar of metonymy, which is fundamentally intricated in metaphor, just as Lacan has taught us to see the rival other that is there "from the beginning" in the constitution of identity . . . .

14. See Freud, "The Infantile Genital Organization," *S.E.* xix, 142.

6

Reading the Phallus

Lacan is frequently accused of phallocentrism, an accusation fairly easy to level at a theorist who proclaims that "the phallus is the privileged signifier."[1] Lacan's defenders do not deny the privilege of the phallus in his system, but they argue that his attackers misunderstand the meaning of the term. The question of Lacan's ideological position—phallocrat or feminist—thus in large part hinges on the meaning of the phallus. That is our concern in this chapter: the meaning of the term "phallus" in Lacan's work and more specifically the text entitled "The Meaning of the Phallus."

Luce Irigaray has accused Lacan of phallocracy.[2] In a recent

---

1. "La Signification du phallus" in *Ecrits*, p. 692; "The Signification of the Phallus," *Ecrits: A Selection*, p. 287. This essay has also been translated as "The Meaning of the Phallus" by Jacqueline Rose in Mitchell and Rose, eds. *Feminine Sexuality*, p. 82. The two translations vary considerably but this unambiguous phrase is identical in both. I will use my own translations, but all quotations from "La Signification du phallus" will have three page references: *E, S, FS*. For a different but related reading of "La Signification du phallus," see chap. 2 of my book *The Daughter's Seduction*, pp. 15–32.

2. Luce Irigaray, "Così fan tutti" in *Ce Sexe qui n'en est pas un*, pp. 83–102. For a discussion of the Irigaray-Lacan polemic, see chap. 6 of *The Daughter's Seduction*.

article, Ellie Ragland-Sullivan takes Irigaray to task for misreading the meaning of the phallus in Lacan: "Irigaray reads Lacan ideologically and substantively. . . . By equating the phallic signifier with patriarchy, she substantivizes the concept biologically such that Phallus=penis=male. . . . [She] fail[s] to see that the phallic signifier is intrinsically neutral."[3] Ragland-Sullivan succeeds where Irigaray "fails." Her article makes it clear that she is able to disintricate the "Phallus" from its identification with the penis and the male. But she does not simply dismiss Irigaray as wrong; she is disturbed by Irigaray's failure. "What I find particularly disturbing in Irigaray's analysis," writes Ragland-Sullivan (p. 10), "is her 'resistance' to getting Lacan 'right.' . . . she misreads Lacan." The use of the psychoanalytic term "resistance"—a use indicated as figurative by the quotation marks—suggests that the misreading occurs in a context in some way like the dynamic of the transference in psychoanalysis. In such a context, the response to misreading would not be simply correction but rather analysis, interpretation, intervention. And if Ragland-Sullivan finds this misreading "particularly disturbing," perhaps Irigaray's reading is not the only one that must be situated in the transferential realm of desire as well as the realm of cognition.

Probably all Lacan's advocates somewhere make the point that his detractors misread him by failing to distinguish the "phallus" from the "penis." Later in her article, Ragland-Sullivan refers to this general phenomenon: "The critic Frederick [sic] Jameson has written that 'many attacks on the Lacanian doctrine of the phallic signifier seem to be inspired by their confusion of the penis as organ with the phallus which is signifier, function or metaphor' (YFS, p. 352)."[4] Ragland-Sullivan

3. Ellie Ragland-Sullivan, "Jacques Lacan: Feminism and the Problem of Gender Identity," SubStance 36 (1982), 10. The capitalizing of "Phallus" is Ragland-Sullivan's. For a different but related consideration of the phallus/penis distinction, see my "Phallus/Penis: Same Difference" in Men by Women, Women and Literature, vol. 2 (New Series), ed. Janet Todd (New York and London: Holmes & Meier, 1981), 243–51.

4. Ragland-Sullivan, p. 12, quoting from Jameson, "Imaginary and Symbolic in Lacan," p. 352.

quotes Jameson to give added authority or generality to her point; she might have quoted many others, critics and psycho-analysts, explaining the attacks on Lacan in like manner. If we look at page 352 of Jameson's cited article, however, we find that the quotation is a false quotation. Jameson never quite said that. In a footnote that spans pages 352 and 353, he writes: "the feminist attacks on Lacan, and on the Lacanian doctrine of the Signifier, which seem largely inspired by A. G. Wilden, 'The Critique of Phallocentrism,' tend to be vitiated by their confu-sion of the penis as an organ of the body with the phallus as a signifier." This example of incorrect quotation, of inexact read-ing, reading that does not attend to the specificity of the sig-nifier—to Jameson's exact words—is noteworthy in the context of a claim that others are reading Lacan incorrectly.

Ragland-Sullivan does not "resist" getting Lacan "right," but at the same time, in that very context, she fails to get Jameson "right." This configuration suggests that "getting Lacan right," or simply reading accurately, particularly where the "phallic signifier" is concerned, may be harder than one would think. (I should add here that after drafting this section I discovered that I had misread Ragland-Sullivan's first name as "Elie," had so noted it in my text and footnotes, even remarking to myself that it was an unusual spelling. Although it appears at the top of every page of her article, only when I happened to glance at the back cover of the journal, did I see, for the first time, that it is spelled "Ellie." Evidently, I am not immune to the difficulty I am describing, this rampant dyslexia which seems to attend reading the phallus.)

Like all parapraxes, Ragland-Sullivan's misquotation can be read as a statement. It even employs one of the classic Freudian techniques amply illustrated in *Jokes and Their Relation to the Un-conscious:* condensation.[5] Jameson sees the "feminist attacks" as "inspired by" Wilden's critique and "vitiated by" the confusion of penis and phallus. Ragland-Sullivan condenses the statement so that the attacks are "inspired" by the confusion itself. Jam-

5. Sigmund Freud, *Jokes and Their Relation to the Unconscious. S.E.,* VIII, 16–45.

eson imagines that feminist criticisms of Lacan must originate in an authoritative male intellectual source and that they are then secondarily spoiled by lack of clear thinking. Perhaps he even refers to the author of the "The Critique of Phallocentrism" as "A. G." rather than "Anthony Wilden" (as found on Wilden's book) in order to cover over the author's maleness. In Ragland-Sullivan's version, a feminist need not have read Wilden to consider Lacan phallocentric. The confusion has become a primary phenomenon, capable of generating an intellectual position.

Ragland-Sullivan goes on to say that "[e]ven though the Lacanian Phallus does not refer to . . . the biological organ, this term does underline the idea that . . . the penian part-object, and the phallic differential function are confused in language" (p. 13). She considers that the "Lacanian Phallus" is a "differential function" and does not refer to the biological organ, the penis. Although she herself does not confuse the two, neither does she treat the confusion as some contingent failing on the part of Lacan's detractors (like that implied by Jameson's word "vitiated"), but rather sees that the confusion inheres in language, in the term "phallus" itself. Even though Lacan might intend the word "phallus" to mean a "neutral," "differential function," because he uses a word that is already in the language, already in use, in the lexicon—Le Petit Robert, for example, defines it as "virile member"—the confusion is inevitable.

In "The Signification of the Phallus," Lacan makes an unusually clear statement differentiating the phallus from the penis: "The phallus in Freudian doctrine is not a fantasy. . . . Nor is it as such an object. . . . It is even less the organ, penis or clitoris, which it symbolizes" (E, 690; S, 285; FS, 79). By negative, diacritical definition, Lacan is at least explicit as to what the phallus is not. Not a fantasy, not an object, but least of all an organ, least of all the penis. We can gather from this progression that it is in fact closer to being a fantasy or an object than to being the penis as organ. It does, however, clearly have a relation to the penis: the phallus symbolizes the penis. But even this link does not constitute a special relation between phallus and penis, for the phallus also symbolizes the clitoris.

As Ragland-Sullivan says, "the phallic signifier is intrinsically neutral": neither on one side nor the other of the sexual divide, it equally symbolizes a male and a female organ, penis or clitoris. And as if to testify to that neutrality, a provocative typographical error appears. The passage just quoted from Lacan is found in the first paragraph of page 690 in *Ecrits*, where it is preceded by one sentence: "The phallus here is elucidated through its function." This sentence is quite obscure, especially compared to the clarity of the negative assertions that follow. The most striking thing about it, at least in the 1966 edition of *Ecrits*, is the first word of the paragraph; the definite article preceding and modifying "phallus" is feminine—"la." In the next sentence the usual, correct masculine article returns, the word "phallus" being masculine in French. If "the phallic signifier is intrinsically neutral," then the signifier "phallus," the word in the language, might be either feminine or masculine, epicene. "In epicene language . . . gender is variable at will, a mere metaphor." This definition of epicene language appears in Mary Jacobus's feminist quest (inspired by Irigaray) for "an alternative version or . . . another model of difference."[6] If the Lacanian phallic signifier is a "differential function," then "La phallus" might indeed intimate an alternative version of difference. A lovely fantasy, a wish-fulfillment: that improper "la," whoever its author, transgresses the linguistic rules of gender and propels us, if but for a moment, into an epicene utopia.

By 1971, when "La Signification du phallus" is reprinted in a paperback selection of *Ecrits*,[7] the momentary feminization of the phallus has been corrected, its masculine article restored. This moment of transgression is not only brief but also extremely hard to read. I must have read page 690 some twenty times over ten years before I noticed the "La," first word of the page, gaily travestying the phallus. It is surprisingly difficult to

6. Mary Jacobus, "The Question of Language: Men of Maxims and *The Mill on the Floss*," *Critical Inquiry* 8, no. 2 (1981), 219; reprinted in *Writing and Sexual Difference*, ed. Elizabeth Abel (Chicago: University of Chicago Press, 1982), p. 49.

7. Lacan, *Ecrits* II (Paris: Seuil, 1971), p. 108.

read the actual word on the page, particularly the improper word, rather than read the word one thinks ought to be there. The reader unconsciously corrects the typographical error, as if the reader were an accomplice trying to cover over the writer's transgressions.

Nonetheless, that illegitimate and expunged "La," barely noticeable, might still have passed on a legacy. Lacan's oft-quoted seminar of February 20, 1973, is entitled "Dieu et la jouissance de ~~la~~ femme."[8] The phrase "la femme" translates literally as "the woman," although here it means the generic entity "Woman," referring to all women. In English it is idiomatic for there to be no article at all preceding a generic category like this. We would translate the title "God and Woman's Ecstasy," except that the correct, idiomatic absence of the definite article deprives the translator of a word to cross out. And so the word "la," usually so insignificant as to be routinely dropped without loss in translation, when crossed through and yet retained can now not be removed without significant loss. Crossed through, it takes on capital importance. In her translation of the title—"God and the *Jouissance* of ~~The~~ Woman"—Jacqueline Rose even capitalizes the "The," contrary to standard English practice for articles in titles, although she does not capitalize the earlier "the" in that very same title. The crossing through of a word usually indicates a correction. Might not this crossed-through, corrected "La," which cannot be removed without cost, in some way recall an earlier incorrect "La" and its subsequent suppression?

The crossed-through "La" of the title refers to a statement Lacan makes in the text of the seminar: "*La* femme can only be written by crossing through *La*. There is no *La* femme, a definite article to designate the universal" (*S* xx, 68; Lacan's italics). The verb Lacan uses for crossing through is "barrer." In "The Signification of the Phallus," he says that when the phallus is un-

---

8. Lacan, "Dieu et la jouissance de ~~la~~ femme" in *Le Séminaire* xx: *Encore* (Paris: Seuil, 1975), pp. 61–71; translated as "God and the *Jouissance* of ~~The~~ Woman," by Jacqueline Rose in *Feminine Sexuality*, pp. 137–48. I will refer to *Encore* as *S* xx.

veiled, which is also when the phallus disappears, "the phallus then becomes the bar [*la barre*]" (*E*, 692; *S*, 288; *FS*, 82). "Barre" is the noun form of the verb "barrer." The "bar [*barre*]" is the line which crosses through words like "la." If the phallus becomes the *barre*, the barred "La" would then be another version of "La phallus."

Immediately after stating in the 1973 seminar that "la" must be written crossed through (*barré*), Lacan voices a complaint that his students do not read him as well as his attackers (in this case, Nancy and Lacoue-Labarthe) and that every one of his students has produced "gibberish regarding the phallus, even though [Lacan] points out to [them] in this *la* the signifier, which despite everything is common and even indispensable."[9] His students do not read him well, and so when they wish to explain or use the Lacanian notion of the phallus, they produce only gibberish. He seems to be offering the necessarily crossed-through "la" as an antidote to his students' inability to read the phallus.

Lacan goes on: "It's a signifier, this *la*." Back in "The Signification of the Phallus," after he says what the phallus is not (fantasy, object, organ), he states directly what it is: "the phallus is a signifier" (*E*, 690; *S*, 285; *FS*, 79). The seminar of February 20, 1973, continues: "It is by this *la* that I symbolize the signifier whose place it is indispensable to mark, which place cannot be left empty." As the translator of this very "la" finds, its "place cannot be left empty" because then there would be no article to cross through. The English translator's "The" has no meaning, in fact its presence distorts the meaning (from generic to definite, specific woman), but it is nonetheless "indispensable," it must be there to bear the mark of the *barre*.

Lacan's seminar continues: "The *La* is a signifier which is characterized by being the only one which cannot signify anything." Three weeks later, in his next seminar, Lacan states that the "phallus as [he] specifies it [is] the signifier which has no

9. *S* xx, 68; *Feminine Sexuality*, p. 144. The complaint about his students not reading as well as Nancy and Lacoue-Labarthe has been elided from the translation.

signified" (*S* xx, 75; *FS*, 152). "La" is the signifier which does not signify anything. "Phallus" is the signifier which has no signified. It would seem then that not only the bar through "La" but "La" itself may be an avatar of the phallus. As for page 690 of *Ecrits,* perhaps the reader might better understand the Lacanian phallus, might better apprehend the phallic signifier, and not simply reduce it to a signified, if—rather than recognize the too-familiar "phallus" there on the page—she read the first word on the page, read the unauthorized, feminine article.

A feeling of exhilaration accompanies my glide from "phallus" to "La." Loaded down with the seriousness of ideological meaning and sexual history, the phallus mires me in its confusion with the male organ. "La" seems to fly above all that in a disembodied ether of pure language, an epicene utopia where "gender is variable at will." But the "La" at the top of page 690 is nearly impossible to read. "Phallus" is still masculine in French, and although I do not believe in a "natural" linguistic gender (*vagin,* vagina, after all, is masculine too), although I am convinced of the arbitrary relation between signifier and signified, the masculinity of the phallic signifier serves well as an emblem of the confusion between phallus and male which inheres in language, in our symbolic order.

My reading here will have to be in some way double. On the one hand, a utopistic attempt to read the "la," to find and reflect on the zones in the text where transgression is inscribed; on the other, a necessary recognition of the substantial weight and incredible resiliency of the symbolic order's phallocentric law. Such a double position is recommended by Jacqueline Rose in her introduction to *Feminine Sexuality:* "Lacan's statements on language need to be taken in two directions—towards the fixing of meaning itself (that which is enjoined on the subject), and away from that very fixing to the point of its constant slippage, the risk or vanishing-point which it always contains (the unconscious)" (*FS,* 43). Rose parenthetically lets us know that the two vectors of language are (1) "that which is enjoined on the subject," that is, the law, the rules of grammar or propriety or identity, and (2) "the unconscious," that which speaks in parapraxes. These, then, constitute our double agenda for reading: if we ignore the rules of grammar and the lexical fixing of meaning we read only flying non-sense; but we repress the material spec- ificity of what is written, which in its peculiarity always carries with it unconscious inscription, if we read only what ought to be there (enjoined meaning) rather than what actually is.

Not only language but also sexuality in Lacan has, according to Rose, a double character: "Sexuality is placed on both these dimensions at once. The difficulty is to hold these two emphases together—sexuality in the symbolic (an ordering), sexuality as that which constantly fails" (FS, 43). The two dimensions of language we find in reading may have their analogue in two opposing directions in sexuality. There is "an ordering" of sexu- ality that corresponds to "enjoined meaning." We might under- stand this as normative sexuality, sexual identity as ordered by phallocentric difference: prescriptive masculine and feminine identity. The other sexual direction, analogous to linguistic par- apraxis, is that which in any subject always falls short of, is inadequate to or in rebellion against, fixed sexual identity.

Beyond suggesting the analogy, Rose does not make clear what precisely is the relationship of sexuality to language. In fact, the awkwardness of the statement "sexuality is placed on both these dimensions at once" suggests that the relation is both important and unclear. Something is normally "in," not "on" a dimension. The phrase "in a dimension" would imply that sex- uality is within, contained by the field of language; the preposi- tion "on," however, indicates that sexuality is something out- side of language, secondarily laid on top of it. It is complicated enough to be "in" two dimensions at once, but the difficulty of sexuality is a greater awkwardness, for it transgresses the en- joined preposition, the grammatically correct relation, in trying to locate itself on a dimension.

Something "placed in a dimension" is safely fixed but some- thing "placed on a dimension" could slip off. The alternatives here—"fixed" and "slip off"—recall the two dimensions of lan- guage. Whether the result of typographical error or imprecision of expression, the statement positioning sexuality "on both dimensions" partakes of the duplicity it describes. There are two directions to the statement: (1) an ordering: it locates sexuality and language, designating their subdivisions; and (2) a failing: the statement "slips away" from the fixing of meaning and from a stable positioning of sexuality through its awkward "on both dimensions."

Although the statement would identify the location of sexuality, the latter's position "on" means it could easily slip off; in other words, its position is precarious. At the beginning of her introduction, Rose makes the point that "Freud's stress on the . . . precariousness of human subjectivity itself . . . was, for Lacan, central to psychoanalysis' most radical insights" (*FS*, 29). For Freud and Lacan, precariousness, the position tenuously on top of, is central, that is to say, well within. If precariousness is central, then in some way "on" is "in." Rose goes on to say that bisexuality is the "sign of that precariousness" (ibid.). Bisexuality renders sexuality difficult in that it holds together in one subject two different directions, two different emphases. By playing around and through these various analogies, I am trying to show the dense intrication of these terms.[10] But the actual relations between the terms seem very difficult to fix. The same duplicity and precariousness seem to hold on various levels of the problem. The collapse of levels, the contagion of difficulty from subject matter to theoretical description, might be understood as a difficulty in separating the "in" from the "on."

The word "precarious" makes two appearances in the introduction of Rose's coeditor, Juliet Mitchell. The first use not surprisingly concerns sexuality. Mitchell writes: "In Lacan's reading of Freud, the threat of castration is . . . what 'makes' the girl a girl and the boy a boy, in a division that is both essential and precarious" (*FS*, 7). This characterization of sexual difference resembles Rose's two emphases of sexuality: an ordering (essen-

---

10. Rose also says: "The phallus can only take up its place by indicating the *precariousness* of any identity assumed by the subject on the basis of its token" (*FS*, 40; my emphasis).

tial) and a constant failing (precarious). Sexual identity, always in the shadow of castration, is always precarious.

On the last page of Mitchell's introduction, "precarious" returns, but this time it is Lacan's "project" itself that is "precarious" (FS, 26). If, as Rose puts it, precariousness is central for Lacan, it is small wonder that his project itself might be precarious, but it is nonetheless interesting to imagine how the problematic nature of his project might link up with the tenuousness of sexual identity, in short, to wonder how the difficulty of Lacan's enterprise, its (near) impossibility, might itself be an effect of the castration complex.

The precariousness of Lacan's project inevitably produces an unsettling effect upon his attempt to "fix the meaning" of the phallus. John Muller and William Richardson, in their reader's guide to Ecrits, state that at a certain point in "The Signification of the Phallus," "the term 'phallus' . . . assumes a new ambiguity, oscillating as it does between its role as signifier and its role as real or imagined organ."[11] In the modesty of their painstaking attempt to read, Muller and Richardson are often good, if naive, readers, able in their acknowledged stance of naivete to see where the emperor might not be clothed. They find that the Lacanian "phallus" "oscillates," it wavers, which is to say, it is precarious.

Muller and Richardson notice a place in Lacan's text where a certain slippage occurs in the "enjoined meaning" of the phallus: "Up to this point, 'phallus' has been used clearly to designate *not* an organ but a signifier. Now Lacan speaks of a 'real phallus' rather than a signifier and the sense is the physical organ of the male" (p. 337). The passage to which they are referring is the following sentence from Lacan: "This ordeal of the desire of the Other, clinical experience shows us that it is not decisive inasmuch as the subject there learns whether he himself [or she herself] has or does not have a real phallus, but inasmuch as he [or she] learns that the mother does not have it"

11. Muller and Richardson, *Lacan and Language,* p. 337.

(E, 693; S, 289; FS, 83). The sentence refers to the "clinical fact" that it is the mother's castration and not the subject's which is decisive for the castration complex, a point Lacan makes very clearly at the beginning of the essay.[12] The question whether or not the subject has "a real phallus," although not the decisive question, does seem to use the term phallus to mean an organ that that subject might have, a "real" organ. Now, defending the purity of Lacan's usage, we might argue that Muller and Richardson misunderstand, inasmuch as when Lacan describes what is "not decisive," what the castration complex is not, he is characterizing a common misprision of the complex. Thus his "real phallus" would be simply an ironic use of the term, his mockery of the way others understand it. So be it. But nonetheless I think that such subtleties of irony never leave their user uncontaminated.

The reader finds Lacan using "real phallus" in a seeming reference to the penis. The effect, as Muller and Richardson put it, is "the slippage between the two senses of 'phallus'" (p. 338). They use the Lacanian term "slippage," thus suggesting that Lacan's language is subject to the effects Lacan describes in his statements on language. When Rose says "Lacan's statements on language need to be taken in two directions—towards the fixing of meaning itself, . . . and away from that very fixing to the point of its constant slippage," we might read that to mean that "Lacan's statements"—his *parole*, his own use of language—need to be taken in these two ways, that his language itself, and not just his theory of language, includes a fixing and slippage. And that we need to read it in both ways.

Rose herself does not much read Lacan in that way. Nor do most of his commentators attend to the slippage in his text; rather, they concentrate on the fixing of meaning. This tendency seems a symptom of transference, to be sure, but a more precise

---

12. "[T]he signification of castration in (clinically manifest) fact takes on its effective import in the formation of symptoms only after its discovery as castration of the mother" (E, 686; S, 282: FS, 76).

analysis might be that perhaps Lacan's theory of language as subjecting the speaker to division and precariousness is so intolerable that the acceptance of that theory brings about a concomitant and unwitting rejection in the form of a belief in Lacan's mastery of language.

As we have seen, Lacan uses the phrase "a real phallus" in a paragraph which discusses the decisive moment when the subject discovers that the mother is "castrated," that the mother does not "have it." That same paragraph ends with a very evocative sentence: "Here the conjunction is signed between desire inasmuch as the phallic signifier is its mark, and the threat or the nostalgia of the lack-in-having [*manque-à-avoir*]" (*E*, 694; *S*, 289; *FS*, 83). From the moment the subject discovers that the mother is castrated, a "conjunction is signed." "Conjonction" (conjunction) is the nominative form of the verb "conjoindre," which Lacan uses a page earlier in a much-quoted sentence that includes some of the same elements: "The phallus is the privileged signifier of that mark where the share of the logos is conjoined to [*se conjoindre à*] the advent of desire" (*E*, 692; *S*, 287; *FS*, 82). The verb "conjoindre" commonly means not only "conjoin," but also "marry." Rose in fact translates this clause as "where the share of the logos *is wedded to* the advent of desire." In the first quotation we are considering, a "conjunction is *signed*": legally binding, a marriage contract between desire and the castration complex. Desire shall henceforth be wed to castration because the phallic signifier is the mark of desire. The resonance between "mark" and "signed" suggests that the "phallic signifier" "signs" the contract on the part of desire. The allusion to a marriage contract here is provocative and links up with other marital and reproductive imagery in this essay; but for the moment, for our purposes, let us concentrate on the two alternative versions of the "lack-in-having," of the castration complex.

Desire can be married to a threat, or it can join a nostalgia instead. If the threat is understood as the male's castration anxiety, fear of losing what he has as the mother lost hers, then perhaps the nostalgia is the female's regret for what she does not have (any longer). Man's desire will henceforth be linked by law to a menace; but woman's desire will legally cohabit with nostalgia: she will not be able to give up her desire for what she can never have (again). A similar alternative appears on the first page of this *écrit* where Lacan asks "why must [man (*Mensch*, the human being)] take on the attributes [of his or her sex] only by means of a threat or even under the aspect of a deprivation?" (*E*, 685; *S*, 281; *FS*, 75). As the context makes clear, Lacan is here talking about "the castration complex in the masculine unconscious [and] *penisneid* [penis envy] in the woman's unconscious" (ibid.). Here, the alternative versions of castration are: a threat or a deprivation. Man is threatened with loss, woman is deprived. Because she feels deprived, her structural attitude is one of envy: she envies what she has not got, the penis. This is pretty standard Freudian stuff, but in the later quotation Lacan uses the word "nostalgia" rather than the more usual "deprivation" or "envy." The characterization of the feminine version as "nostalgia" is remarkable and perhaps even unique.

This unusual word, "nostalgia," certainly not a recognized term in the Lacanian lexicon, makes one other appearance in "The Signification of the Phallus." Toward the beginning of the essay Lacan writes: "The fact remains that the now abandoned discussion on the phallic phase, when we reread its texts surviving from the years 1928–32, refreshes us by the example of a doctrinal passion, to which the degradation of psychoanalysis, consequent upon its American transplantation, adds a value of nostalgia" (*E*, 687; *S*, 283; *FS*, 77). Psychoanalysis used to have something which now it has lost. When we see what it had, we (psychoanalysts in 1958, Lacan, readers of the early texts) feel nostalgia. We feel a desire for what we (psychoanalysis) once had but now, in our "degradation," have lost. What we had and lost is "passion."

How might this "nostalgia" resemble the nostalgia that attends desire consequent to the discovery of the mother's castration? According to Freud as read by Lacan, the discovery of the mother's castration is what brings an end to the phallic phase.[13] The phallic phase is henceforth irretrievably past, a fit object for nostalgia. We might then say that the 1928–32 discussion on the phallic phase that evokes Lacan's nostalgia constitutes for him, so to speak, the phallic phase of psychoanalytic theory. In this way the "American transplantation" would function as an analogue to the discovery of the mother's castration. The fate of psychoanalysis in America shows that it is not (is no longer) phallic but "degraded," castrated. In terms of this analogy, it is noteworthy that Lacan's reaction to the discovery that his "alma mater" is degraded follows the feminine model: he is not threatened, he is nostalgic.

Yet if by means of this analogy we gain an understanding of one level (the history of psychoanalytic theory) because of its resemblance to another (the development of the female subject), let us also use the analogy in the other direction. My point is not to reduce theory to subjectivity but to see the ways the levels intertwine and thus to understand both better. In the sentence about the degradation of psychoanalysis, nostalgia results from a "rereading," a look back at the texts of an earlier period. Nostalgia is not the natural effect of the development of psychoanalysis but rather accompanies a moment of retrospection, of the *Nachtrag* that Lacan recalls in the brief introduction to "The Signification of the Phallus." Nostalgia here is a regret for a lost past that occurs as a result of a present view of that past moment. If we apply this temporal logic to the other example of nostalgia in this text, the result is that the nostalgia of penis envy does not simply accompany the moment of castration, but rather is a retroactive effect.

It is not that the girl experiences loss but rather that, looking back from a later perspective on some past before the "decisive discovery," she feels regret. This logic might resolve certain questions which pose themselves as to whether she is "literally

13. "Now it is my view that what brings about the destruction of the child's phallic genital organization is this threat of castration": Freud, "The Dissolution of the Oedipus Complex," *S.E.* xix, 175.

castrated." For the boy, the moment of loss is always an immi-
nent future, a threat, an anticipation; for the girl there is no
moment of loss, but loss is inferred on the basis of a retro-
spective view that sees the past as fuller than the present. Something must have been lost. Taking together the case of the girl
and the boy, the retroaction and the anticipation, we might say
that the moment of loss is "toujours en attente ou en retraite,"
always to come or gone by, which is, let us remember, how
Jean-Michel Palmier describes the meaning of Lacan's *Ecrits*.[14]

There are two meanings given for "nostalgie" in the dictionary (*Le Petit Robert*): "(1) State of withering or of languor caused
by the haunting regret for one's native land, for the place where
one lived for a long time: homesickness. (2) Melancholy regret
(for something elapsed or for what one has not experienced);
unsatisfied desire." Freud says of homesickness that it can be
understood psychoanalytically as a longing to return to the
womb, that the lost homeland is the mother's womb.[15] If we
understand the nostalgia resulting from the discovery of the
mother's castration in this way, then the discovery that the
mother does not have the phallus means that the subject can
never return to the womb. Somehow the fact that the mother is
not phallic means that the mother as mother is lost forever, that
the mother as womb, homeland, source, and grounding for the
subject is irretrievably past. The subject is hence in a foreign
land, alienated.

Nostalgia is also the "melancholy regret" that something is
over, something one has not experienced. Hence Lacan's nostalgia for the psychoanalysis of the years 1928–32 is a regret that he
did not know psychoanalysis firsthand before its "degradation." This interpretation may provide a clue about an oddity in

14. Palmier, *Lacan*, p. 13.
15. Freud, "The Uncanny," *S.E.* xvii, 245: "There is a joking saying that
'Love is home-sickness'; and whenever a man dreams of a place or a country and says to himself, while he is still dreaming: 'this place is familiar to
me, I've been here before,' we may interpret the place as being his mother's
genital or her body."

the dates he gives for the discussion of the phallic phase. In another *écrit*, written the same year as "The Signification of the Phallus," Lacan says that "the question of the phallic phase in woman . . . was the rage in the years 1927–1935."[16] Certainly 1935 is a more usual date to give for the end of this debate; some of the most important texts were in fact written after 1932. In 1932 Lacan published his thesis. Although it contains bits of psychoanalytic theory, it is the thesis of a psychiatrist. In 1936 Lacan participated in his first international psychoanalytic congress. Perhaps in the context of his "nostalgia," he gives 1932 rather than 1935 because in 1932 he was not yet fully a member of the psychoanalytic community whereas by 1935 he was. Using the earlier date would establish that Lacan was too late for psychoanalysis's phallic phase.

Both the dictionary definitions of "nostalgie"—homesickness and regret for something past—prove useful in the understanding of Lacan's text. However, there may be another definition which, though appended to the second—"melancholy regret"—finally suggests a more radical notion of nostalgia. The dictionary appears to give two definitions—each with two parts. The second part of the first, "homesickness," is a sort of summary of the rest of the definition and is thus preceded by a colon. The second definition seems to have a construction homologous with the first; the second part seems to be, like "homesickness," a summary but is in fact preceded by a semicolon, therefore constituting another definition but one whose independence is barely marked. That "third" definition—"unsatisfied desire"—may have a lot to do with the Lacanian theory of desire. The Lacanian subject is castrated, that is to say, deprived of the phallus, and therefore can never satisfy desire. Desire, for Lacan, is an offshoot of that part of need which "finds itself alienated" (*E*, 690; *S*, 286; *FS*, 80), which is to say "homesick." Thus desire is "paradoxical" (ibid.), which is to say it cannot be satisfied. The quotation illustrating this last mean-

16. Lacan, "Directive Remarks for a Congress on Feminine Sexuality" in *Ecrits*, p. 727; translated in *Feminine Sexuality*, p. 88.

ing in the dictionary is from Antoine de Saint-Exupéry, a contemporary of Lacan (born one year earlier): "Nostalgia is the desire for the indefinable something [*le désir d'on ne sait quoi*]."

In translating the Saint-Exupéry quotation, I was troubled by the phrase "on ne sait quoi." That construction is "so French" it often almost appears untranslated in English, as if the phrase itself were indefinable. I say almost because it is actually its close relative "je ne sais quoi" that is the resident alien in our language. I found that phrase—"je ne sais quoi"—in my French-English dictionary under the entry for "quoi," and it listed "the indefinable something" as the English equivalent, which I then chose to use, momentarily suppressing the difference between "je" and "on." On reflection, "on ne sait quoi" seems to suggest something slightly more radically indefinable, unknowable, something that not only a specific subject, a "je," would not know, but something no subject would know, no subject could define. That the phrase translates as "the indefinable something" seems particularly appropriate. The quotation from Saint-Exupéry is, after all, at least in form, a definition: "Nostalgia is . . . [*La nostalgie c'est . . .*]." He defines nostalgia as the desire for what cannot be defined. And then of course this quotation appears in the dictionary, the very storehouse of definitions. As a quotation it is presumed to illustrate the use of the word, but in this case the quotation actually provides an additional definition, one which ties the word to the impossibility of definition.

The etymology of "nostalgia" informs us that "nostos" in Greek means "return." Both the principal definitions relate to a return, the first in the wish to return to a place (Vienna, perhaps? see Chapter 4 above), the second in the wish to return to a time (see Chapter 3). In *Beyond the Pleasure Principle*, Freud suggests that all drives are drives to return to an earlier state. In *Three Essays on the Theory of Sexuality*, he states that the object of desire is always refound, always an object of previous satisfaction.[17] But the "third" definition of "nostalgie" finally suggests

17. *Beyond the Pleasure Principle*, S.E. xviii, 37–38; *Three Essays on the Theory of Sexuality*, S.E. vii, 222. For an interesting discussion of this see Laplanche, *Vie et mort en psychanalyse*, p. 36; trans., p. 19.

a transgression of return: a desire ungrounded in a past, desire for an object that has never been "known." Reading Saint-Exupéry's definition of nostalgia in a psychoanalytic context, one might say that desire does not know its object, has no (conscious) idea of its object, because of repression. But of course the repressed was once conscious and so the desire is for a return to an object whose definition, idea, knowledge is only contingently unavailable to the subject. That is the usual notion of repression, which would implicate return even in the most radical case of nostalgia: the desire for "je ne sais quoi," the desire for what the "je," the ego does not know. But what of the "on ne sait quoi"? What if the object of desire were not yet an "object" but an indefinable something, radically indefinable, the result of primary repression (*Urverdrängung*)? The primary repressed was never present to consciousness, nor to any "je," but is primordially and structurally excluded. There is no past state that was once present to which one could return, even in fantasy. The return cannot be imagined because one does not know the "object." What Lacan calls desire is precisely the result of this primary repression and yields up a nostalgia beyond *nostos*, beyond the drive to return, a desire constitutively unsatisfied and unsatisfiable because its "object" simply cannot ever be defined.

The word "Urverdrängung" makes two appearances in "The Signification of the Phallus." The first is in a sentence from which I quoted in the discussion above on the meaning of nostalgia: "What thus finds itself alienated in the needs constitutes an *Urverdrängung* by being unable, by hypothesis, to articulate itself in the demand; but which appears [*apparaît*] in an offshoot [*rejeton*], which is what presents itself in man as desire (*das Begehren*)" (*E*, 690; *S*, 286; *FS*, 80). The "Urverdrängung," primary repression is that part of needs which is left out in the articulation of a demand, and which man experiences as desire. "Rejeton" literally means "offshoot," but commonly means "child." What Lacan calls desire is an offshoot, a child of primary repression. Both Sheridan and Rose translate the verb "apparaît," a cognate of "appear," as "reappears." They add the sense of a return, of desire as a return of the proto-repressed. But in the original text it is not a return; the only appearance of the primary repressed (which cannot appear as such) is its appearance as desire. Born of an alienation, primal repression cannot appear any place, cannot have its own place, cannot have a home. There is no primary appearance of proto-repression, only its secondary appearance, which is thus not a return, as desire. Desire, the offshoot, is thus always, from the beginning, an orphan child.

Perhaps the most difficult part of this Lacanian sentence is the phrase "par hypothèse," literally, "by hypothesis." Rose translates this phrase as "by definition": the "*Urverdrängung* cannot, *by definition*, be articulated in demand." The definition of primary repression is that which is left out of articulated language. Or we could say that the primal repressed is that which cannot be defined and therefore cannot be articulated: articulated language necessitating definition. The "by," the "par," here is ambiguous: (1) the "Urverdrängung" can be defined as that which cannot be articulated, and (2) the "Urverdrängung" cannot be defined and thus cannot be articulated. Not only ambiguous, but antithetical: the second meaning calls the first into question. But of course "definition" and "hypothesis" are two quite different operations. At least one of the meanings of "by definition" suggests that the "Urverdrängung" is definable and even defined. But, although the "par" in "par hypothèse" does have a similar ambiguity, neither sense implies a definability. Or rather, since the sentence is itself a quasi-definition, the "by hypothesis" emphasizes that this definiton is only a hypothesis. By Lacan's working hypothesis, a speculation in psychoanalytic theory, the "Urverdrängung" is that which cannot be articulated. This can be only a hypothesis because the "Urverdrängung" cannot be articulated, that is, it cannot be defined. Sheridan renders this reading in his translation: "an *Urverdrängung*, an inability, *it is supposed*, to be articulated in demand." Because of its ambiguity, the phrase might also mean that the proto-repressed cannot hypothesize itself and thus cannot articulate itself. This reading implies a theory of articulation in which "the needs" are projected into language by means of anticipation, that is, by hypothesis: a theory resembling Lacan's mirror stage, for example. It is not definition that is the necessary condition for language but rather hypothesis, anticipatory speculative definition. But still there is something that cannot even hypothetically be defined, although, of course, in its other reading this sentence is its hypothetical definition, its articulation with other terms.

This radically indefinable something, finally not even definable by hypothesis, is named by Lacan only in German. Both English translations give an English equivalent ("primal repression") in parentheses following the German word, but Lacan never provides a French version of "Urverdrängung." In his text, it remains "alien," not fully articulated with the rest, homesick. In contrast, the sentence closes with another German word ("das Begehren"), but this one appears with its French equivalent, "désir." Desire is what "presents itself," it "appears," whereas the "Urverdrängung" never appears (in French).

"Urverdrängung" reappears toward the end of this *écrit*, albeit in a different grammatical form: "what is living of [the subject's] being in the *urverdrängt* finds its signifier in receiving the mark of the *Verdrängung* of the phallus" (*E*, 693; *S*, 288: *FS*, 82). I must admit to finding this sentence particularly enigmatic. Ten years ago when reading it for the first time I was so puzzled as to place a question mark in the margin next to it. I am not yet prepared to answer that question, but let us nonetheless try to work this sentence.

"Urverdrängung" appears here as past participle, "urverdrängt." It is soon accompanied by another word in German, "Verdrängung": the latter, signifying the ordinary, "secondary" sort of repression, is a noun, a process presently going on, whereas the "urverdrängt," the primal repressed, is a past participle, an already completed process. After proto-repression has already taken place, that which is thus primarily repressed can be signified. But its signifier is not its own, but is the "mark of the (secondary) repression of the phallus." Just as desire constitutes the only appearance of proto-repression, an already alienated, secondary, displaced appearance, so the only signifier of the primary repressed is an alienated, displaced mark, the mark of a secondary repression.

The words "living" and "being," not exactly typical Lacanian terminology, are here associated with the primal repressed. If the repression of the phallus comes to share a signifier with the proto-repression of the "living" and the "being," then the phallus comes to be metaphorically linked to life and being. Not the phallus as a full presence, as a defined thing, but the repressed phallus, the veiled phallus, the uninterpreted phallic symbol also symbolizes but secondarily and in alienation what is living in the subject's being which cannot be articulated in language.

Thus it is not that the phallus is some sort of original, primal, living real, but in its repression—better, in its "Verdrängung," the foreign word offering another level of veiling—it comes into association with these. A page earlier Lacan says, "One can . . . say that [the phallus] is by its turgidity the image of the life flow [*flux vital*] inasmuch as it passes in generation." One can say that the phallus is the image of the life flow, of what is living but not articulated. One can say that but, as Lacan puts it in the very next sentence, "[such] remarks only veil the fact that it can play its role only when veiled." To talk of the phallus as image of the life flow, to talk about the phallus as representing "what is living in the subject's being," is to veil a fact, is to repress, to veil the fact that the phallus functions, functions as a signifier of the primal repressed, only when it is veiled, in its "Verdrängung."

Muller and Richardson declare, in a discussion of this passage of the text: "We are left to guess at some vague sense to the myriad reasons that attempt to explain the importance of the phallus as a symbol throughout the history of human culture. In any case, the final reason given by Lacan for choosing the phallus as signifier of all signifiers is less problematic: 'By virtue of its turgidity, [the phallus] is the image of the vital flow . . . transmitted in generation.' That much, at least, is clear" (p. 336).

Most of Lacan's explanations of the phallus's privilege are "vague," that is to say, veiled. But "the final reason . . . , at least, is clear." And by being clear it, of course, veils the fact that the phallus functions veiled. Clarity, it turns out, in the logic of the phallus, is not the absence of a veil, but the veiling of a veil. When Muller and Richardson find clarity, they neglect the fact that the following sentence asserts that such remarks veil a fact as well as the fact that Lacan begins the statement with "one can say [*on peut dire*]." This is not a Lacanian explanation of the phallus's meaning but something "one can say."

Rose, on the other hand, is very careful to separate Lacan's sense of phallus from what "one can say." Referring to this passage from *Ecrits*, she writes: "he constantly refused any crude identification of the phallus with the order of the visible or real and he referred it instead to [the] function of 'veiling' " (*FS*, 42). In her introduction, Rose connects what "one can say" with Lacan's statements that such remarks veil the phallus's veiling, a connection Muller and Richardson fail to make. They mistakenly hear what "one can say" as something Lacan does say. Rose is careful not to. Perhaps too careful. Rose translates "on peut dire" as "one might say," moving the utterance into the conditional mood. In the French the assertion is possible ("one can"); in the translation it is a conditional possibility, slightly more attenuated, less likely.

The translation of "on" as "one" is strictly correct but perhaps too correct. The first word of the text of "The Signification of the Phallus" is the pronoun "on." On this initial occasion as well as on several others in the first half of the text, Rose and Sheridan both translate "on" as "we," a perfectly acceptable translation. The text begins: "On sait—we know, one knows, that the unconscious castration complex has the function of a knot." In the translation the "on" that knows this is a different subject from the "on" that can see the phallus as the image of the life flow. The first "on" is we, Lacan, his fellow psychoanalysts, the good guys. The lack of consistency in the translation of "on" silently interprets so as to separate the subject who knows from the subject who can say such "unLacanian things" as that the phallus is the image of the life flow. Yet in French it is the same subject, "on."

Which is not to say that the subject is whole, undivided, but that the division is not so neat. Lacan says that the id must not be thought of as a second ego,[18] that the two agencies must not be thought of as two egos, or two subjects, inhabiting the same psyche. That would be a reassuring representation of a much more precarious division. The split personality, however scary it is, is a domestication of, a defense against, the subject's division. The "on" in Lacan's text is divided, but the division never creates two clearly separable subjects with different names, different identities. The subject that knows cannot be separated from the subject that can mistake the phallus for a penis (with its "turgidity" and its fluids that participate in "generation"). After all, even the "on" that is us, the good guys, knows something rather equivocal. "The Signification of the Phallus," which Rose calls "the most direct exposition of the status of the phallus" (FS, 74), begins: "We know [on sait] that the unconscious castration complex has the function of a knot [une fonction de noeud]." "Noeud," the French word for knot, is a well-known crude term for "penis."

18. Lacan, Le Séminaire II.

7

The Dream of the Dead Author

Composed in 1960, "The Subversion of the Subject and the Dialectic of Desire in the Freudian Unconscious" is the latest of the papers selected for the English translation of the *Ecrits.* Muller and Richardson comment that it is "probably the most enigmatic of this particular collection."[1] According to the dictionary, an enigma is "an obscure riddle." At the very beginning of their book, Muller and Richardson posit that Lacan's writing is a rebus, that is, a kind of riddle (pp. 2–3), and as they begin the final chapter of their reader's guide to *Ecrits,* they prepare the reader to face "the most enigmatic" of rebuses, the riddle of riddles. In psychoanalytic lore, the great solver of riddles is Oedipus, who answered the riddle of the sphinx.[2] Faced with the riddle of riddles at the end of *Ecrits: A Selection,* the reader is in the complex position of Oedipus confronting the sphinx. At that point in his story, Oedipus had already killed his father, but he did not yet know it.

In "Subversion of the Subject" Lacan mentions Oedipus several times, but seems to dismiss the Oedipus story as merely a

1. Muller and Richardson, *Lacan and Language,* p. 356.
2. For an interesting discussion of Oedipus the riddle-solver, see Cynthia Chase, "Oedipal Textuality: Reading Freud's Reading of *Oedipus,*" *Diacritics* 9, 1 (1979), 54–68.

myth: "Of no more use than that of the accursed apple, except for the fact that . . . it is perceptibly less cretinizing" (*E*, 820; *S*, 317). In the Judaeo-Christian tradition, the myth of the "accursed apple" explains and epitomizes human suffering; Adam mythically represents the condition of fallen man, a fall into knowledge, suffering, and death. Freud goes back to the ancient Greeks to find a story that will likewise serve to represent man's unhappy fate. Every man has an Oedipus complex; Oedipus mythically epitomizes the desiring subject. In "Subversion of the Subject," Lacan treats the Oedipal story as myth but uses another story from Freud—not a myth but a dream—to illustrate the subject's fate: a dream of a dead father who did not know that he was dead.

We have here a transformation of Oedipus, of Oedipus the riddle-solver whose father was dead but he did not know it. In both cases, a dead father; but the transformation highlights another element. From the story to the dream, what changes is the subject who does not know: in the story the son does not know; in the dream it is the father. In both cases it is a question of a subject of knowledge who does not yet know. Oedipus solves the riddle and after that (not immediately, of course) this dauntless seeker of knowledge comes to know of his father's death. That knowledge is tragic: it blinds him and then kills him. In the dream, as long as the father does not know he is dead, he can be present, but as soon as he knows, he will disappear; as soon as he knows, he is lost: "He did not know . . . A little more and he knew, oh! would that that never happen" (*E*, 802; *S*, 300). Oedipus and the dreamt, dead father, as well as Adam of course, are all at one point ignorant of something knowledge of which will bring their downfall.

According to Lacan, "the coordinates [of the Freudian myth of Oedipus] come down to the question . . . what is a Father?— It's the dead Father, answers Freud" (*E*, 812; *S*, 310). Oedipus answers the riddle with "man"; Freud answers with "the dead Father." Lacan shifts the emphasis from the deadly answer to the deadliness of an answer, of a knowing that kills. Whereas the myth of Oedipus stresses the importance of the dead father, Lacan emphasizes the relationship of knowledge. The subject at stake in "The Subversion of the Subject," the subject Lacan is subverting, is the subject of knowledge, the subject who knows.

In Freud's telling of the dream, it is clearly the father who does not know: "his father was nevertheless dead, only did not know it [*der Vater doch schon gestorben war und es nur nicht wusste*]."[3] Freud's German refers not simply to "his father" as does the English but to "the father" (*der Vater*). The father was dead, only did not know it. The dream edges into the archetypal, an image of the generic dead father, Freud's "answer" to the riddle.

When Lacan recounts the dream in "Subversion of the Subject," it is harder to be sure who does not know: "A dream reported by Freud . . . offers us, linked to the pathos which sustains the figure of a deceased father by being that of a ghost, the sentence: He did not know that he was dead" (*E*, 801–2; *S*, 300). As we pass from Freud to Lacan, the subject of the verb "know" is no longer "der Vater," but only a nearly impersonal "il," "he." Nor is it grammatically necessary that the first "he" refer to the same subject as the second "he." Oedipus, facing the sphinx, did not know his father was dead; he did not know that he was dead.

In Freud we read "was dead, only did not know it"; the two verbs are conjoined and knowing comes second. In Lacan knowing is the primary verb; being dead is a subordinate clause, depends on the knowing. In his seminar of February 12, 1964, Lacan says: "the true formula of atheism is not that *God is dead*— in the very act of basing the origin of the function of the father on his murder, Freud is protecting the father—the true formula of atheism is that *God is unconscious*."[4] In the place of the dead God, dead Father, Lacan offers us the unconscious father, un-

---

3. Freud, "Formulations Regarding the Two Principles in Mental Functioning," *S.E.*, xii, 225 ("Formulierung über die zwei Prinzipieren des psychischen Geschehens," *Gesammelte Werke*, viii, 238). My quotations from this article modify the *Standard Edition* translation, following the translation by M. N. Searl that appears in Freud, *General Psychological Theory*, pp. 27–28.

4. *Le Séminaire* xi, p. 58; *Four Fundamental Concepts*, p. 59; henceforth referred to as *S* xi and trans.

conscious, unaware, the father who does not know. And so we go a step beyond Freud (and Nietzsche), who in the figure of the dead father is still "protecting the father."

Lacan's one-sentence account of the dream separates it into two elements, the figure of a dead father returned as a ghost and a "sentence." One element is an image full of pathos; the other is a linguistic structure whose subject is the third-person masculine singular pronoun. And in Lacan's account, these two elements are not equally weighted. However much the reader might be intrigued by ghosts, pathos, and dead fathers, that lurid, Hamletic image is a distraction from the grammatical main point of the sentence. Lacan's sentence, reduced to its principles, reads: "A dream . . . offers us . . . the sentence." The sentence may be "linked" to the pathetic figure, but the pathos is secondary, a subordinate construction. The only direct object is "the sentence."

Lacan's primary focus here is not on the father's ghost but on the rather skeletal sentence: "He did not know that he was dead." A nearly impersonal subject, knowing, being, and death. A paradigmatic structure without modifiers: no details, no image, no figures, no pathos. Whereas "the figure" places us in the dramatic tradition of Sophocles and Shakespeare, "the sentence" would seem to be in the sparer tradition of Descartes. Lacan distills a new *cogito* or an anti-*cogito*, much darker but with the same stunning simplicity: rather than I, he; in the place of thinking, ignorance (not knowing); the loss of the *ergo*, loss of logical causality; and in the place of being, being dead.

The structure of Lacan's account of the dream—privileging "the sentence," subordinating the pathos—embodies a certain direction in his work which prefers linguistic structures (the symbolic order) over the juicier, more dramatic figures of the imaginary register. This is the direction that would gladly separate the phallus from the penis, as we saw in the last chapter, gladly free the symbolic from the delusions of the imaginary, as I discussed in Chapter 2. Psychoanalysis would move in the direction of science—first, linguistics and later, mathematics—by ridding itself of the mythic, the dramatic, the figural, and the anecdotal, in short by ridding itself of literature. According to Shoshana Felman, literature "inhabits" psychoanalysis: "the key concepts of psychoanalysis are references to literature using literary 'proper' names—names of fictional characters (Oedipus complex)."[5] Such an interiority of literature to psychoanalysis threatens to ruin the latter's claim to scientific authority. The structure of Lacan's account of the dream would seem to represent a drive to evict literature from this key position.

The prominent and complex "graphs" and "algorithms" in "Subversion of the Subject" exemplify this drive toward scientificity. Commenting on the most difficult graph in the essay, Catherine Clément remarks: "It is here that Lacan's poetic invention pretends to adorn itself with the plumes of a scientific peacock."[6] For Clément, who prefers his poetry and myths, Lacan's scientificity is the weak side of his work: "we will wonder if all these apparatuses, all these equations, are not facades to hide the shabbiness of a thought at its wit's end" (p. 210). Clément chooses Lacan the poet over Lacan the scientist, "because Lacan understands the rhythm of myth better than mathematics" (ibid.). For myself, I am enormously gratified by Clément's judgment. As someone with a literary rather than a scientific education, I find Lacan's stories and poetry more sympathetic, more pleasurable, and easier than his graphs and later "mathemes." Sorely tempted, I do not, however, feel free simply to dismiss the latter. Even if Clément is right and Lacan's science is a failure, his drive toward science is part of the work. On the other hand, I would also strongly protest against any attempt to purify Lacanian science of stories. Agreeing with Felman, I would say that, at least in Lacan's writing, literature inhabits psychoanalysis.

Let us look again, more closely, at Lacan's account of the dead father dream, the structure of which seems at first glance to embody Lacan's preference for philosophy and linguistics over literature. "A dream reported by Freud . . . offers us [*nous*

5. Felman, "To Open the Question," p. 9.
6. Clément, *Vies et légendes de Jacques Lacan*, pp. 206–7; trans., p. 178.

livre] . . . the sentence." The transitive verb "livrer" means to deliver something to someone—for example, to deliver what the buyer ordered—but also to confide something to someone, as in confiding a secret, and also to turn something or someone over to the authorities—for example, to deliver the culprit into the hands of the law. The sentence is our captive, our possession, our thing that we can work upon. But although it is "ours," is given over to us, it is still not free from prior entanglements.

The verb "livrer" has a contradictory relation to freedom. Since it means to put something in someone's possession, it implies a submission, a lack of freedom of the thing delivered, but, etymologically, it means to deliver in the sense of to liberate and derives from the Latin *liberare*. The ambiguous resonance of freedom and bondage is echoed in the very next word of Lacan's sentence; "liée," meaning tied, bound, attached. "A dream . . . *nous livre, liée* (offers us, tied) . . . the sentence." The sentence is in bondage. "Liée" is resonant with Lacan's frequent use of the concept or image of the knot. For example, the same page of *Ecrits* which begins with the dream account and the word "liée" ends with the statement that "desire is tied [*se noue*, is knotted] to the desire of the Other" (*E*, 802; *S*, 301). As we saw at the end of the last chapter, "The Signification of the Phallus" opens with the declaration that "the unconscious castration complex has the function of a knot." By the mid-seventies, Lacan is trying to theorize the interrelation of the symbolic, the imaginary, and the real in terms of the topology of knots, and he continues trying to understand and make "Borromean Knots" from the early seventies until his death in 1981.[7] In contrast to the urge to disentangle the symbolic from the imaginary, another persistent strain in Lacan's work is formulating their relation as a knot. The symbolic and the imaginary, along with the real, are tied together (*noués, liés*).

7. See for example, *Le Séminaire* xx, *Encore*, pp. 107–23 and Clément, pp. 215–17; trans., pp. 185–87.

"A dream . . . delivers to us, tied to the pathos which sustains the figure of a deceased father by being that of a ghost, the sentence." The sentence the dream "delivers to us" is, first of all, "liée" to the pathetic figure of the dead father. Even before it appears, "the sentence" is already bound to an old story. Lacan's reader must pass through the drama of the ghost tale with all its affect before she can get to the anti-*cogito*. The sentence cannot disintricate itself from the burden of the father's ghost.

"What is a Father?—It's the dead Father, answers Freud . . . and . . . Lacan takes it up again under the heading of the Name-of-the-Father" (*E.* 812; *S*, 310). Freud's answer still "protects the father." Lacan would recast the answer as the "Name-of-the-Father," that is, as a name, a signifier, a member (the key member) of the symbolic order. Lacan would "deliver" the lurid drama of the dead father over to the symbolic order. But as the knotty paragraph under consideration here suggests, the Name-of-the-Father is bound by its legacy from the imaginary figure of the dead Father. The linguistic models, the symbolic structures that Lacan distills from Freud cannot simply be disengaged from the myths and drama to which they are tied.

The subordinate clause that tells us what the sentence is tied to appears in lengthy and distracting complexity before we ever get to "the sentence," holding up the delivery of what is "delivered to us." Whereas "the sentence" is straightforward and easy to read, the clause that precedes it is involuted and difficult to figure out: "tied to the pathos which sustains the figure of a deceased father by being that of a ghost [*liée au pathétique dont se soutient la figure d'un père défunt, d'y être celle d'un revenant*]." My translation is in fact an interpretation, less ambiguous than the original French, an interpretation based upon Freud's account of the dream which made it possible for me to "solve" Lacan's enigmatic statement. I am guessing as to the sense of "d'y être," as to the logical relation between the figure of the dead father and the figure of the ghost. "Which sustains" is also much simpler and more straightforward than "dont se soutient." This clause which interrupts the progress from verb to direct object, which derails the delivery of the principal point, threatens to haunt the reader who cannot finish deciphering it and thus cannot properly lay it to rest.

Moreover, what Lacan calls "the sentence" appears in Freud not as a separate sentence but as a subordinate clause. The complete dream account in Freud's article reads: "his father was again alive and he was talking to him as of old. But as he did so he felt it exceedingly painful that his father was nevertheless dead, only did not know it." In Freud's text, Lacan's "sentence" actually finds itself grammatically subordinate to, literally dependent upon, an extremely painful feeling. This is surely the pathos Lacan mentions. The so-called sentence is actually a clause dependent on pathos. Although Lacan has it that the pathos sustains the figure, it in fact sustains that sparse anti-*cogito*.

Lacan introduces and situates the dream of the dead father thus: "A dream reported by Freud in his article: *Formulations Regarding the Two Principles of Mental Functioning*," whereupon the reader is directed to a very rare footnote: "*G.W.*, VIII, p. 237–238."[8] Lacan's reader often wishes for but is seldom given precise references. Frequently Lacan will mention a Freudian phrase or dream or concept in passing without deigning to note in which work it is found. Sometimes he does not even tell us that something is taken from Freud. But here he even gives the page reference. No enigma here; everything is revealed. As in a dream, the reader finds her wish fulfilled: volume VIII, pages 237–238.

In reality, the dream appears only on page 238, although the paragraph in which it is found does begin on page 237. Any hint or foretaste of the dream is strikingly absent from page 237, even from the very paragraph which on the next page will include the dream. In fact, nothing in the article prepares the reader for the dream's sudden appearance in the middle of the penultimate paragraph, on the last page of the article, page 238. With all the

8. *Ecrits*, 802; *Ecrits: A Selection*, 300 n 6 (the note is on p. 325). "*G.W.*" is the standard abbreviation for *Gesammelte Werke*.

precision of the footnote, the reader still ends up with a small unanswered question.

Or maybe two. Freud not only reports this dream in the article Lacan names but also includes it, from 1915 on, in *The Interpretation of Dreams,* in a section on absurd dreams. This dream appears there in the context of a discussion of dreams of "loved ones" who are dead. All the dead "loved ones" in the example dreams just happen to be fathers.

Here is the dream as we find it in *The Interpretation of Dreams:* "*His father was alive once more and was talking to him in his usual way, but* (the remarkable thing was that) *he was nevertheless dead, only did not know it.*"[9] This version is actually closer to Lacan's account than the one he cites. The subject who is dead and does not know it is here the masculine singular pronoun, "er." Most remarkably, in this version the pathos is missing; there is no mention of the dreamer's "feeling it extremely painful." In place of the pathos is the parenthetical remark that this was remarkable: no longer painful, just "remarkable," a change from intense affect to intellectual curiosity. The italics are Freud's, his usual means of presenting dreams, but the parenthetical remark is not in italics, is not a part of the dream text proper. In the dream text itself, Lacan's "sentence," although still not a separate sentence, is an independent rather than a dependent clause, introduced by a coordinating ("but") rather than a subordinating conjunction. The parenthesis actually serves to isolate, package, and "deliver the sentence" to the reader. This version would seem to be much more sympathetic to Lacan's retelling, yet nothing in Lacan's text even acknowledges its existence. The reader is instead carefully directed to a version that inscribes "the Father" in the sentence and makes that "sentence" dependent upon pathos.

Just before he brings up this dream, Lacan is once again (see Chapter 4 above) commenting on the Freudian sentence "Wo Es war, soll Ich werden [Where it was, I should come to be]." He then goes on to recount the dream and to tell us exactly *wo es*

9. Freud, *The Interpretation of Dreams,* S.E. v, 430.

war, but like the whereabouts of the unconscious id (*Es*) the location of the dream remains somehow puzzling. In giving, on this rare occasion, an exact reference, Lacan manages to give both too much—237 and 238—and too little—only one of its two locations. His exclusive mention of one site (seemingly the less likely of the two) as well as his inclusion of an extra page would seem to insist that the reader return *wo es war*, back to the article, "Formulations on the Two Principles of Mental Functioning." Not just back to Freud's account of the dream, but to what precedes it, for example, to page 237.

The article is primarily about the difference between the pleasure principle and the reality principle. There is a list of eight formulations that follow from the idea that a reality principle supersedes the infantile reign of the pleasure principle. The dream appears in the paragraph headed by the numeral 8. The eighth formulation is that unconscious processes are not under the reign of the reality principle but proceed "just as happens . . . under the supremacy of the old pleasure-principle." Then Freud offers a word of caution to the explorer who would venture to go *wo Es war:* "one must . . . never allow oneself to be misled into applying to the repressed creations of the mind the standards of reality." That is where page 237 ends. There seems to be some danger. One could be misled, one could get confused about reality, ascribing it to figments of the imagination. "The repressed creations" tempt us to stray, but one must never allow oneself to be misled.

The paragraph continues, proceeding onto page 238: "One is bound to employ the currency that prevails in the country one is exploring; in our case it is the neurotic currency. For example, one may try to solve such a dream as the following." The reader then comes upon the dream in question, the dream of the father who did not know he was dead. Prefaced only by the briefest "for example." An example, chosen at random. Why this dream rather than any other dream, or rather than a neurotic symptom, since we are speaking of "neurotic currency"? Any symptom, parapraxis, or dream ought to be equally able to illustrate the reign of the pleasure principle and the disregard of reality in unconscious processes? And why is the dream or any example at all here? This is the only example, the only anecdote, in an otherwise metapsychological text. The vivid detail of this example distracts the reader from the more general discussion of mental functioning. Freud warns us not to be misled and yet the dream that follows the warning threatens to divert the reader from the metapsychological discussion it ought to serve. The dream and the interpretation with which Freud follows it bring the text to its close and risk captivating the reader's imagination, making him forget the rest of the article and remember only this illustration of the last of eight points deriving from the main point.

"For example, one may try to solve such a dream," try to solve such an enigma, such a riddle. Freud follows the account of this dream with his solution: "No other way leads to the understanding of this seemingly senseless dream than the addition of 'as the dreamer wished,' or 'as a result of his wish,' after the words "that his father was nevertheless dead'; and the further addition of 'that he wished it' to the last words." "No other way," let us not be misled, there is only one way that "leads to the understanding" of this dream. If we would "solve . . . this seemingly senseless" dream, we must recognize that dreams function according to the pleasure principle, that is, according to the dreamer's wish. The pleasure principle is the reign of wishes, unbridled by reality. The father was dead, only did not know that the dreamer wished it. What the father does not know, according to Freud, is that in this dream we are under the sway of the dreamer's wishes, under the rule of the pleasure principle. If we would solve this riddle, let us not be misguided, let us not be ignorant like the father.

Freud concludes his solution: "It is thus a matter of the familiar case of self-reproaches after the loss of a loved person, and in this case the reproach goes back to the infantile significance of the death-wish against the father." Once we use neurotic currency, once we recognize where we are, in the land where wishes hold sway, the seemingly senseless reveals itself as familiar. And, in the wake of Freud, what is more familiar than the dead father, Freud's answer to the riddle? Oedipus is not named in this text, but Oedipus is the "proper" name of this infantile death-wish. No longer the solver of riddles, Oedipus is the solution.

Two years before the composition of "Subversion of the Subject," Lacan discusses this dream in his seminar and suggests that "to interpret the dream at this [Oedipal] level" is a way "of identifying with the aggressor which would be a form of defense."[10] The son did not kill his father but watched him die, painfully and slowly. To interpret that he died "as the dreamer wished," even according to a forbidden, guilty Oedipal wish, allows the subject to identify with the aggressor, allows the subject authorial intention, posits him as generator of meaning for this death, and is a mode of defense against something more awful: "Everything that can here be defined as a determinable desire is inadequate [*en défaut*] compared to the gaping which the father's death opens up" (*Désir*, 270). The Oedipal interpretation, the universal myth Freud offers to close off the dream, which also brings to its conclusion the article in which the dream appears, upholds the formulation about the sovereignty of the pleasure principle. Lacan's suggestion that the Oedipal interpretation is a defense implies that there is something beyond.

Nine years after he wrote "Formulations on Two Principles," Freud wrote that the reality principle "does not abandon the intention of ultimately obtaining pleasure." The reality principle is merely a modification which makes the pursuit of pleasure more practical, but the goal, "obtaining pleasure," remains the same. He wrote this in a work he called *Beyond the Pleasure Principle*.[11] Although in 1911 he speaks of the replacement of the

10. Jacques Lacan, "Le Désir et son interprétation," compte-rendu par J. B. Pontalis, *Bulletin de Psychologie* 13, 5 (1959), 270. This is an account of the seminars of November 12, 19, and 26, December 3, 10, and 17, 1958, and January 7, 1959. These seminars have not yet been published, and these accounts are not in Lacan's words but written by Jean-Baptiste Pontalis. Henceforth referred to as *Désir*.

11. *Beyond the Pleasure Principle*, S.E. xviii, 10.

pleasure principle by the reality principle, in this 1920 work, though he mentions the reality principle in the first chapter, he quickly dismisses it as a mere modification of the pleasure principle. Moreover, he goes on to use the latter as a term to include both principles in the rest of this work, in which he is tracking something "beyond the pleasure principle" *and* beyond the reality principle, here not itself considered to be beyond the pleasure principle at all. He tracks this "something beyond" through various manifestations of repetition. His exploration starts by considering the repeated dreams that return patients again and again to traumatic scenes. In 1911, when he still believed that everything could be formulated in terms of the opposition between the pleasure and the reality principles, he undercuts the force of his argument by ending with a distracting illustration: "For example, one may try to solve such a dream as the following. A man who had . . . looked after his father through a long and painful illness up to his death, informed me that in the months following his father's decease he had *repeatedly dreamt* as follows:" (emphasis mine).

The dream Freud uses to illustrate the reign of the pleasure principle is a dream that the dreamer experiences as "exceedingly painful," and it is a repeated dream. In *Beyond the Pleasure Principle*, he explains that the repetition of painful experiences in dreams and children's play is an attempt to master an exceedingly painful event by taking over the position of author of this event. "At the outset he was in a *passive* situation—he was overpowered by the experience: but, by repeating it, unpleasurable though it was . . . he took on an *active* part" (p. 16). This, I believe, is what Lacan means in his seminar when he considers the Oedipal interpretation of the dead but ignorant father "an identification with the aggressor." The dream Freud chooses, seemingly at random, to illustrate the sovereignty of the pleasure principle in unconscious processes could well be an illustration of the repetition compulsion and the death drive that are beyond the pleasure principle.

When Lacan retells the dream in *Ecrits*, he ambiguously assigns the ignorance and the death: "He did not know that he was dead." Either dreaming son or dead father can be represented by the pronoun subject. Indeed, perhaps the most radical version of the Oedipal conflict/identification would be the attempt to determine which subject—father or son—had the right to the masculine pronoun "he." In the seminar, Lacan suggests that the Oedipal myth is a "lure," an "imaginary fixation" that covers over a more radical confrontation that occurs in this dream. At stake is not only the Oedipal desire for the father's death (imaginary, within the pleasure principle) but a more radical death drive or "death desire." "The death desire is here the desire not to wake up to the message: through the death of his father, he is henceforth confronted with his own death" (Désir, 270).

The Oedipal wish is not only a wish for the father's death, but also and as centrally a wish to be in the father's place. Yet that identification risks collapsing into the aggression so that if the father, as wished, dies, the Oedipal complex involves an identification with the dead father, an image of one's own death. If one tries to think at one and the same time the desire for the father's death and the desire to be in the father's place, one risks facing the desire for one's own death.

Among the identificatory elements in the dream, Lacan in the seminar points to the dreamer's "exceedingly painful feeling" which repeats the father's "painful illness." "His father's pain, the subject knew it, but what he does not know, is that that pain as such, he is in the process of assuming it, of taking it on" (Désir, 270). The subject identifies with the father's pain and, like the victim of trauma in Beyond the Pleasure Principle, repeats the pain in an attempt to master it, to bind it, to understand it, to give it meaning.

Freud repeats the dead father dream in The Interpretation of Dreams, this time placing it among other dead father dreams. This particular dream is the last of several such dreams, and the section then closes with the following observation: "In other dreams in which the dreamer associates with dead people, the following rule often helps to give us our bearings. If there is no mention in the dream of the fact that the dead man is dead, the dreamer is equating himself with him: he is dreaming of his own death."[12] Once more, as at the other site of this dream, there seems to be a danger of getting lost. "One must . . . never allow oneself to be misled," and this "rule" will help "give us our bearings," will prevent us from being led astray. In the dream we are considering it is not exactly that there is no mention that the father is dead; rather, the dreamer explicitly avoids mentioning to his father that he is dead. This seems to be a more dynamic, dramatized version of the issue. The mention of death is a manifest source of anguish; it is an explicit concern of this dream.

If we allow Freud's "rule" to orient us, we might say that by preserving his father's ignorance, the dreamer wishes to make it a dream of his own death. As odd as this might seem, it corresponds to something Lacan says in his commentary on the dream in "Subversion": "Rather than have him know, 'I' would die" (E, 802; S, 300).

Following his formulation of the "rule," Freud continues: "If, in the course of the dream, the dreamer says to himself in astonishment, 'why he died ever so long ago,' he is repudiating this equation and is denying that the dream signifies his own death." If we continue the application of the rule to our dead father dream, we might compare the "astonishment" here with the parenthetical comment above which found it "remarkable" that the father was nevertheless dead. The astonishment there replaces an earlier feeling of extreme pain. Freud's two accounts of the dream (1911 and 1915) correspond to the two moments of the general rule. In the first version the dreamer feels extreme pain, like the father's extreme pain: that is, the dreamer experiences the pain of dying, identifies with the dead man. In the second version, no pain, no identification, just astonishment (whose? the dreamer's? Freud's?).

In the general rule we find knowledge and ignorance as two different moments of a dream. First the dream does not know (mention) the dead man is dead, then later it does know ("A

12. *The Interpretation of Dreams*, S.E., v, 431.

little more and he knew," Lacan says of the oneiric dead father). In the dream we are discussing, knowledge and ignorance are apportioned not to two moments but to two different characters: the father does not know, the son does. Of course, one might say that, in a certain patrilineal order, the son is a later moment of the father.

The terms "knowledge" and "ignorance" are quite confusing here. When the dream knows (mentions) that the figure is dead, then the dreamer does not recognize, does not know that he himself is dead. When the dream does not know (mention) that the figure is dead, then the dream-interpreter can know that the dreamer is dead. In any case there seems always to be a knowledge somewhere with an accompanying ignorance. There is, of course, the question of the relationship between the dreamer (ignorant) and the dream-interpreter (knowing) and how that might be like the relation between the ignorant father and the knowing son.

In "Subversion of the Subject," Lacan dramatically interprets the dream in question, emphasizing the topic of knowledge through four uses of the verb "know" in one short paragraph: "He did not know . . . A little more and he knew, oh! would that that never happen! Rather than have him know, 'I' would die. Yes, that is how 'I' come there, there where it was: who then knew that 'I' was dead?" (E, 802; S, 300). Lacan here is speaking in the role of the dreamer. The dream-interpreter identifies with the dreamer, continues the dream text. Freud, too, seems to mingle his voice with that of the dreamer, to intervene in the dream text with his parenthetical "the remarkable thing was." We might want to consider how the dream-interpreter's identification with the dreamer repeats the dreamer's identification with the dead father. In both cases a subject comes to be *wo es war*. The dream-interpreter by her very function knows what the dreamer does not know, and what the dream-interpreter knows is some truth about the dreamer. Is this not exactly the situation of the son who knows that his father is dead although the father does not know it?

In my translation of Lacan's paragraph, I have placed the first-person singular pronoun in quotation marks. Sheridan in his translation puts it in italics, although at other points in this text he uses single quotes, around "I." Although Muller and Richardson make no mention of Sheridan's italics in this paragraph, on three different occasions in their notes to this *écrit* they would correct Sheridan by stating "The French does not have quotes around *I*" (pp. 397, 406, 410). It is true that the French text neither italicizes nor places in quotes the word "I," but it does something Muller and Richardson do not note, something that is impossible to translate because of a peculiarity of English. In this paragraph and elsewhere in the essay, Lacan capitalizes the initial j of the French first-person singular pronoun "je." Unlike its English counterpart, that word is normally not capitalized. Neither Sheridan nor I can find a successful translation of this gesture, but it is important to note that this is not an ordinary use of the first-person pronoun, but some slight subversion of the subject.

Two interpretations of the capitalization occur to me. (1) It repeats Freud's capitalization of "ich" in "Wo Es war, soll Ich werden," which makes the word (as we saw in Chapter 4 above) somewhere between the normally uncapitalized German pronoun and the Freudian noun we translate as "ego" since, in German, nouns are always capitalized. (2) It makes the word "I" a proper noun, a name, rather than a shifter. In a sentence quoted above, Lacan says, "What is a Father?—It's the dead Father, answers Freud . . . and . . . Lacan takes it up again under the heading of the Name-of-the-Father." Lacan here refers to himself not by a first-person pronoun but by a proper noun, just as he refers to Freud. Lacan is talking here about the Name-of-the-Father and he refers to himself by his patronym (and not, for example, by his full name, which would include his given name, Jacques). He is also talking about his repetition of something Freud said. Lacan here, in some way, comes to be where Freud was, but he does not come there as "I" but as "Lacan."[13]

"Yes, that is how 'I' come there, there where it was: who then

13. Clément mentions this: pp. 201–2; trans., p. 174.

knew that 'I' was dead?" Freud's general rule for the interpretation of dead father dreams suggests that the dreamer put himself in the place of the dead man, suggests that "I," the subject,
come to be there where It, the thing, the no longer person become dead thing, was. But the use of this rule is followed by a
denial, an ignorance of the identification of the subject with the
dead thing. Who knew that I was dead? What subject could
know? I can know that he is dead, but I cannot know that I am
dead. The subject that is dead cannot know. "I" can come there,
wo es war, but my arrival there is accompanied by a questionable,
indeterminable subject of knowledge. Questionable just as it is
questionable what "Je" signifies, what its relation to "je" is. The
subject who knows ("who?") cannot be the same as the subject
who is dead ("I").

There is a knowledge of the subject's death, a knowledge
implied by Freud's general rule, but who knows that knowledge? It is a knowledge that belongs to no subject. In *Ecrits*, just
a page after Lacan tells the dead father dream, he describes just
such a knowledge, a knowledge whose subject is unaware of it:
"But it is a question of something else in Freud, which is certainly a knowledge [*savoir*], but a knowledge [*savoir*] which does
not entail the least cognizance [*connaissance*] in that it is inscribed
in a discourse of which . . . the subject who wears under his
hair its codicil condemning him to death, knows neither the
meaning nor the text nor in what language it is written nor even
that it was tattooed on his shaven scalp while he was sleeping"
(*E*, 803; *S*, 302).

A distinction between *savoir* and *connaissance* runs through the
first part of "Subversion of the Subject." The two words can
both be translated as "knowledge"; the distinction between
them does not exist as such in the English lexicon. In this sentence, where they are explicitly contrasted, Sheridan keeps
them both in French. Lacan is here distinguishing between a
biological instinct, which is a *connaissance* without *savoir*, and
what we find in Freud, which is a *savoir* without *connaissance*.
Connaissance in this essay is associated with psychology and its
perception of the person as a unified whole with natural devel-

opmental cognitive states. *Savoir* is associated with Hegel, desire, and language. *Connaissance* is an unmediated experience; *savoir* is intricated with discourse.

In the sentence just quoted, let us note the codicil that condemns the subject to death without his knowing it. This could be read as another version of the dream Lacan discusses but a page earlier. The subject of the codicil "did not know that he was dead." The knowledge exists as a text, an *écrit*, inscribed on the body of the subject, like hysterical symptoms. The Freudian unconscious subjects us to a knowledge we cannot read but which we nonetheless carry with us and which spells our death. This is what Freud names the death instinct in *Beyond the Pleasure Principle*. The death instinct is a knowledge within us, a knowledge of our own path to death, but a knowledge we are not cognizant of, do not recognize, a knowledge within us that we do not know, condemning us to death.

There is a typographical error in this sentence as it appears in the original edition of *Ecrits*. In the phrase "inscribed in a discourse," the word "inscribed" (*inscrit*) is missing its "s," and so we actually read "incrit." If we take seriously the "something else in Freud," that word "incrit" would bespeak a knowledge without cognizance. What does "incrit" mean? "The subject . . . knows neither the meaning . . . nor in what language it is written." I find myself, in the spirit of the passage, wondering where the s went and why. My interpretation wants to get to *wo "s" war*.

Besides being a homonym for the Freudian *Es*, "s" is probably the most important letter in Lacan. He uses it to stand for the signifier, the signified, the symbolic, and the subject. When we look at the various graphs in "Subversion of the Subject" we find a lot of different s's, including a barred S ($) which represents the subverted subject, the one who does not know that he is dead. Such barring represents a crossing out of something that is erroneous, something that should not be there. The thing barred is still there but later will be erased. The barred subject is like the father in the dream: momentarily present but the dreamer's knowledge of his death crosses him through. Soon he will disappear. Lacan refers to this as the "fading subject," still there but on its way to disappearing. The barred subject does not yet know that he is dead. If he knew, he would not just be crossed through (marked for future erasure) but actually gone. Not $, but the absent s of "incrit." The missing s is the knowledge of the subject's death, but "who knew that 'I' was dead?" Who is the subject of a typographical slip? Like any symptom or dream, the absent s is a text of knowledge without cognizance.

A few pages earlier, Lacan poses the problem of "the correct way to answer the question: Who is speaking? when what is at issue is the subject of the unconscious. Since that answer could not come from him, if he doesn't know what he's saying, nor even that he's speaking, as the entire experience of analysis teaches us" (E, 800; S, 299). Lacan does not answer the question of who is speaking, that is, who is the subject of the unconscious, who intends typographical errors, but he goes on to speak of the "effects of fading" ("fading" is in English in the original French text) which "lead us to the borders where the lapsus and the joke, in their collusion, become confused" (E, 800–801; S, 299). These "effects of fading" are the "subversion" of the classical, transparent subject of knowledge, the subject who can answer with his name or the first-person pronoun to the question "Who is speaking?" The difference between a joke and a Freudian slip is generally understood to be whether the speaker intends the effect or not, whether the speaker has cognizance of the knowledge inscribed in his utterance. Yet the "subversion of the subject" means that we can no longer distinguish clearly between the intended joke and the unwitting slip.

Lacan's *Ecrits* pose that very problem. We read at those "borders" and constantly wonder if the name Lacan can answer for the knowledge inscribed in the text. We read *Ecrits,* as finally we read any text, for knowledge. And when we find knowledge, we inevitably ascribe it to the "subject presumed to know," that is, we presume there is a subject who knows the knowledge. Lacan's "subversion" of the subject of knowledge makes exceedingly precarious the position of the scholarly reader who

depends upon the assignment of knowledge to a knowing subject. The subject of the knowledge in *Ecrits* is subject to the
"effects of fading." There is a subject there, a certain Lacan, but
he is constantly fading, eluding our perception, on the verge of
disappearing.

In contemporary literary theory we speak easily of the death
of the author, meaning that there is no subject who intends and
guarantees the meaning of the text. But Lacan's theory and writings lead us not to a dead author, but to something more haunting, more ambiguous and disconcerting, to a fading author, one
who is still precariously there, like the father in the dream. The
author is dead but does not know it.

The codicil which condemns the subject to death was inscribed on his scalp while he was sleeping. "Dormait" (was
sleeping) is the last word of the long and vivid sentence about
unconscious knowledge, the last word of the paragraph. A text
of unconscious knowledge impressed on our head while we
sleep reminds us that while we sleep we dream. In his discussion of the dead father dream in his seminar, Lacan enigmat-
ically states, in a sentence I quoted above: "The death desire
here is the desire not to wake up to the message: through the
death of his father, he is henceforth confronted with his own
death." When I discussed this sentence, I commented on the
second half, but the idea of "not waking up to the message"
does not explicitly relate to anything else in Lacan's reading of
the dream and strikes the reader as puzzling. Now, however,
we might say that like the "codicil" on the scalp, the "message"
here is also that of the subject's own death. In order to continue
not to recognize that knowledge, the subject wishes not to wake
up, wishes to continue sleeping.

In *The Interpretation of Dreams*, Freud states that, besides the
major purpose of satisfying unconscious wishes, dreams con-
sistently have another purpose: to avoid waking. We incorpo-
rate a disturbing stimulus like the ringing of an alarm clock into
a dream rather than recognize it and wake up. Lacan discusses
this other purpose of dreams in his seminar of February 12,
1964: "We see here arise, almost for the first time in the *Traum-*

deutung, a function of the dream which is, in appearance, second—the dream here is only satisfying the need to prolong sleep" (*S* xi, 56–57; trans., 57). The word "here" repeated twice in this sentence refers to the very beginning of the last chapter of *The Interpretation of Dreams*—chapter vii, "The Psychology of the Dream-Processes." Unlike the rest of that major work, this chapter is not about the interpretation of dreams, but is a metapsychological discussion of "mental functioning." But though it includes very few dream narratives, it begins with a dream which, according to Lacan, "of all those that are analyzed in this book [*Interpretation of Dreams*], has a fate apart" (*S* xi, p. 35; trans. 34).

Here is Freud's account of that dream:

> A father had been watching beside his child's sick-bed for days and nights on end. After the child died, he went into the next room to lie down, but left the door open so that he could see from his bedroom into the room in which his child's body was laid out, with tall candles standing round it. An old man had been engaged to keep watch over it. . . . After a few hours' sleep, the father had a dream that *his child was standing beside his bed, caught him by the arm and whispered to him reproachfully: "Father, don't you see I'm burning?"* He woke up, noticed a bright glare of light from the next room, hurried into it and found that the old watchman had dropped off to sleep and that the wrappings and one of the arms of his beloved child's body had been burned.[14]

The father must have perceived the light of the fire from the next room in his sleep. But he did not wake up immediately. Rather than wake up, he incorporated the real perception into a dream. Freud asks why he dreamed rather than woke. The dream serves two purposes: to prolong the child's life by a few moments and to prolong the father's sleep by those same few

14. *The Interpretation of Dreams*, S.E. v, 509: emphasis Freud's.

moments. Of the father dreamer here, one could even more appropriately say what Lacan says of the son dreamer: "The desire here is the desire not to wake up to the message."

For Lacan, the context of this dream is triply one of sleep: "everyone is sleeping, the one who wanted to get a bit of rest, the one who could not keep up the wake, and the one about whom, undoubtedly before his bed, some well intentioned person must have said—*One would say that he's sleeping*" (*S* xi, 58; trans., 59). "Everyone is sleeping," says Lacan, and he links the three figures further by using the same pronoun, *celui*, "the (masculine) one." An identification is set up between the father, the old man, and the child: all these (masculine) figures are sleeping. Child, father, old man: classically, the three ages of man, the scene verges on a universal *tableau*, so that when Lacan says "everyone" is sleeping, "everyone" may in fact mean *everyone*. Another look at Lacan's formulation, however, reveals a difference between the last sleeper and the first two. The first two are verb subjects (*celui qui*, the one who); the last figure is only an object (*celui dont*, the one about whom). The child's sleep exists only as a wishful misperception, as a kind of dream. Joining the father's desire to sleep and the desire for the child to be still alive is the wish that the child be (only) sleeping.

This dream of the dead child haunts my reading of "Subversion of the Subject." Not that there is any mention of it in this *écrit*—nothing that could even be construed as an allusion to it. I reread the essay in order to begin thinking about what I would say in this final chapter of my "book on Lacan." As I read his account of the dead father dream, I immediately thought of the dead child dream. I was sure that I had somewhere read a joint interpretation of these two dreams, discussing their common denominators. As I worked on this chapter, I made several frantic attempts to find that discussion, all to no avail. I found interpretations of the dead child dream and others of the dead father dream but no text that examines the two together. My memory of the discussion had a vividness that convinced me I had read it recently so, over and over again, I paged through all the psychoanalytic books I had read or reread in the last year, all to no avail. I wanted to use this joint interpretation but felt I could not unless I could find its source. I have—at least momentarily—given up, without being able to determine whether I am symptomatically forgetting or overlooking the source or whether I only imagined reading it. I have decided nonetheless to present this double reading of the two dreams without being able to tell you what scholarly ethics demand I tell you: who is the subject of this knowledge? who is speaking? what "I" can legitimately come to be where this knowledge was?

In both cases, the dreamer has nursed a dying relative who is now dead but appears in the dream as if alive. The father-son relationship would also seem to be at stake in both. The most striking similarity, however, is that, regardless of who is dead, it is always the father who does not know. In the first case the father does not know of his own death. In the second the father is reproached for not seeing, for not knowing that the child is burning. A composite reading creates an impression of the father as site of blindness and ignorance.

The father does not recognize death, pain, danger. But perhaps also, the father does not recognize desire. "Father, don't you see I'm burning?" could recall the poetic tradition of burning with desire as well as the religious tradition of burning with sin. The dreams of the father's ignorance would then bespeak a wish for the father to be ignorant of the child's desire. Toward the end of "Subversion of the Subject" Lacan describes "the image of the ideal Father" as "a father who would close his eyes on desires" (E, 824; S, 321). The ideal father is the one who does not see that "I" am burning.

According to Lacan, this ideal image "is a neurotic's fantasy" which is to say that, like a dream image, it bespeaks an unconscious wish. He continues the description: "The Father wished for by the neurotic is clearly, it can be seen, the dead Father. But just as much a Father who would be perfectly the master of his desire." The ideal Father is dead, and the Oedipal child fantasizes that death because that death would signify a mastery of desire. The dead are beyond desire.

Sheridan translates one of the sentences just quoted as "The neurotic's wished-for Father is clearly the dead Father." This translation is smooth but it achieves its grace at the expense of a phrase. It leaves out the expression "il se voit," which I translate as "it can be seen." Sheridan probably leaves this out because it seems a repetition of the word "clearly" (*clairement*), which precedes it. But in its redundancy it highlights the visual imagery that is more latent in "clearly" and resonates with "would close his eyes" earlier in the description. Lacan is, after all, talking about the "image" of the ideal Father: an image is something one can see.

The awkwardly redundant "il se voit" disrupts the flow of the sentence. Although its meaning echoes the sense of "clearly," its effect is to make the sentence less clear, to muddy the transparent identity between subject and predicate, to trouble the passage to the dead father. "Il se voit" literally means "he sees himself." The first meaning of "se voir" we find in the dictionary is "see one's own image," accompanied by the example "see oneself in a mirror." The phrase thus might even represent a sort of mirror stage, disrupting the development of the sentence.

Who sees himself in the image of the dead Father? Grammatically it could be the Father or it could be "the neurotic," most recent masculine noun in the sentence ("Le Père souhaité du névrosé est clairement, il se voit, le Père mort"). This rejoins Lacan's reading of identification in the dead father dream and resonates with something Lacan says in the following sentence: "But just as much a Father who would be perfectly the master of his desire, which would be worth as much for the subject." Although the last clause is somewhat ambiguous, Sheridan interprets it to mean "and the same can be said of the subject." In other words, if the Father could master his desire, then the subject could master his. Thus if the wish for the father's death is a wish that the father would master his desire so that the subject could do the same, then it is a wish for the subject's own death. Freud's death drive, we will recall from *Beyond the Pleasure Principle*, is a drive to reduce stimulation/tension to zero, that is to say, since desire provides stimulation/tension, a drive to rid the subject of desire.

But the transparent glass of fatal identification cannot be seen.

The neurotic sees himself in the image of a Father who would close his eyes. If the image in the mirror has its eyes closed, that image cannot be seen, for the viewer would have to close his eyes to produce that image. A certain eye-closing, whether of sleep or respectable death (the dead must have their eyes closed so we can bear to look at them), a certain blindness, inserts itself into the identification with the dead Father, allows it to function.

Another small accident befalls the Lacan passage we are presently considering. In the phrase "a Father who would be perfectly master of his desire," the word "perfectly" (*parfaitement*) is marred by a typographical error. We actually read "parfaitemdnt." The letter which spoils the sentence's perfect mastery is a lower case d, which in the graphs of this essay represents desire.[15]

The ideal reader would not see the "d," would close his eyes on desire, and would read *parfaitement*, would read perfectly, would read a discourse mastered by intention. The ideal reader does not want to "wake up to the message," but wants to prolong his sleep, even if in his sleep he is condemned to death.

If the dead Father is a neurotic fantasy, then what of the current literary vogue of the dead Author? After all, there is a long tradition linking the Author to the Father. Is the image of the dead author a reader's fantasy of perfect mastery? A fantasy for the critic who would identify with such mastery as reader-writer? Is "the death of the author" a defense against something more threatening—a fading author, for example, an author who is neither wholly present nor master of desire?

The dead child provides a retort to the dead father. In his discussion of the dead child dream, Lacan says: "no one can say what the death of a child is—except the father *qua* father—that is to say, no conscious being. For the true formula of atheism is not that *God is dead*—in the very act of basing the origin of the function of the father on his murder, Freud is protecting the father—the true formula of atheism is that *God is unconscious*" (*S* XI, 58; trans., 59). Lacan assimilates Freud's dead father to the

15. *Ecrits*, pp. 814–17; *Ecrits: A Selection*, pp. 311–15.

death of God and sees both as defenses against true atheism. I would add the death of the author to that of God (and) the Father. Freud's murder of the father protects the father image, for the dead father is the ideal father, perfect master of desire. But the dead child, the dream Lacan says is in a different category from all Freud's other dreams, leads us to the unconscious father (the father is here the dreamer), unconscious God, unconscious Author, fading subject of desire.

In fact, the source of the dead child dream, the answer to the question "who is speaking?" in this dream, is not known to Freud, who introduces the dream thus: "It was told to me by a woman patient who had herself heard it in a lecture on dreams: its actual source is still unknown to me. Its content made an impression on the lady, however, and she proceeded to 're-dream' it, that is, to repeat some of its elements in a dream of her own."[16] Who is speaking? an unknown unconscious, an expert on dreams, a woman patient. A lady hears this dream when she goes to a lecture, exercising her desire for knowledge about dreams. She re-dreams the dream: she comes to be *wo es war*. She identifies with the unconscious father, the unidentified author so that, says Freud, "she might express her agreement with it" presumably in transferential dialogue with the Father of Psychoanalysis, himself an expert (and lecturer) on dreams.

Like the "lady re-dreamer," I am haunted by the dead child dream, troubled by a memory of a text whose "actual source is still unknown to me." When Freud says "still unknown" we must presume he still wants to know, has not yet given up trying to ascertain who is speaking. Proclaiming the death of the author asserts that one does not care, is not at all troubled by the still unknown source. My frantic and repeated searches hardly constitute a proper burial for the unknown scholar. In honor of Freud's woman patient, this critical reading of Lacan would like to be a re-dreaming: "that is, to repeat some of its elements in a dream of her own."

The dead father dream is still a version of Oedipus. But the dead child dream might rouse us to something else. In that

16. *The Interpretation of Dreams*, S.E. v, 509.

dream it is not the light but the child's utterance that wakes the father, an utterance which Freud and Lacan point out must be a repetition of something the child actually said, for example, when he was feverish: "Father, don't you see I'm burning?" When the child says "Father, don't you see," the father opens his eyes and sees.

Lacan calls this child a "son," but Freud refers to "him" only as "das Kind" (the child). There is no indication of the child's gender in Freud's text. Lacan assimilates this child to a masculine Oedipal identification, which would make the dream a mirror image rather than a re-dreaming of the dead father dream. But the unanswerable question of the child's sexual identity clouds the mirror. That child whose sex remains to be determined might open up the eyes of the reader who has closed them in identification with the dead Father Author.

Where and why does the subject find the image of the ideal Father? "In fact," says Lacan, "the image of the ideal Father is a neurotic's fantasy. Beyond the Mother, the real Other of demand whose desire one wishes she would calm (that is, her desire), there is outlined the image of a father who would close his eyes on desires" (E, 824; S, 321). The fantasy of the unseeing father is a move beyond the mother in response to the wish that the mother would calm her desire. The dead or blind father would be perfectly master of desire, of the mother's desire, of desire for the mother.

At the end of the page of *Ecrits* which begins with the dream of the dead father, as I noted earlier, Lacan describes the "Freudian relation of the subject to knowledge" by means of "the dialectic of desire": "desire is knotted to the desire of the Other [*le désir de l'Autre*], but . . . in that loop lies the desire to know" (E, 802; S, 301). The subject wants the real Other to calm her desire, wants the ideal Other to be blind to desire, because the subject's desire is inextricably knotted up with the Other's desire,[17] and the

17. Lacan specifies that the ambiguous *désir de l'Autre* which can be read both as the Other's desire and desire for the Other is here to be read as a subjective genitive: "it is *qua* Other that he desires" (E, 814; S, 312).

subject would calm (reduce the tension/stimulation of) her own desire. But in this knot, which the subject wants to untie, is the desire for knowledge. If the subject's desire comes from the Other, the subject does not know what she desires but must learn it from the Other. The desire to know what the Other knows, so as to know what one desires so as to satisfy that desire, is the drive behind all quests for knowledge. Outside the knot, there is no desire for knowledge and thus no impetus to know. We read because we desire to know, and so reading must lie within the knot where the subject's desire is intricated with the Other's. We read to learn what the Other (what the Author) knows, to learn what are his desires, in the hope of understanding and satisfying our own. Outside that knot, we do not read, we close our eyes in identification with the ideal Father who has mastered all desire, including the desire to know. We close our eyes and do not read because we no longer want to know.

The reader who wants to read without or beyond desire would identify with a dead Author and read with his eyes closed. In the present book, as I have been reading Lacan, Lacan has literally died. But, as in the dream that has been the subject of this chapter, Lacan "was alive once more and was talking in his usual way but he was nevertheless dead, only did not know it." To read as if Lacan were simply dead would be to protect his mastery and protect myself from desire in reading. Lacan, the author of the text I have been reading, cannot calm his desire, but in fact provokes mine. I cannot, however, have him, cannot satisfy my desire to know, in any lasting or universal way. For example, the present chapter at most "tears off a piece" of Lacan. It does not consider much more than one paragraph of this very complex and enigmatic *écrit*.

As I close my book on Lacan I feel that he and I are neither properly dead nor properly married (the only true endings for books). Desire is not yet calmed. I do not possess him, to either marry or bury. He is still fading, not faded yet. But my eyes are open. If I have not perfectly mastered Lacan, at least I can read the d in perfectly, the letter of desire which spoils the perfect mastery of the dead author.

POSTORY

The day after I started my final revisions of this book, when I got to work in the morning, I was talking with Jean Lile, Administrative Assistant at the Center for Twentieth Century Studies. I told her that I thought the book was good, and I suddenly remembered that the night before I had had a dream about Lacan. I did not and do not remember it very clearly. I saw Lacan and he was alive. There was no mention in the dream that he was actually dead. He was going to read my manuscript. He was very nice to me, very approving of my work. I think I described to him what I was doing in this book, and I had a sense that he approved, that I was doing the right thing. I was very happy.

Bibliography

Barthes, Roland. *S/Z*. Paris: Seuil, 1970. [*S/Z*, trans. Richard Miller. New York: Hill & Wang, 1974.]

Bell, Susan Groag, and Mollie Schwartz Rosenhan. "A Problem in Naming: Women Studies—Women's Studies?" *Signs: Journal of Women in Culture and Society* 6, 3 (1981), 40–42.

Chase, Cynthia. "Oedipal Textuality: Reading Freud's Reading of *Oedipus*." *Diacritics* 9, 1 (1979), 54–68.

Cherki, Alice. "Pour une mémoire." In *Retour à Lacan?*, ed. Jacques Sédat. Paris: Fayard, 1981.

Clément, Catherine. *Vies et légendes de Jacques Lacan*. Paris: Grasset, 1981. [*The Lives and Legends of Jacques Lacan*, trans. Arthur Goldhammer. New York: Columbia University Press, 1983.]

Creech, James. "'Chasing after Advances': Diderot's Article 'Encyclopedia.'" *Yale French Studies* 63 (1982), 183–97.

Derrida, Jacques. *La Carte postale*. Paris: Aubier-Flammarion, 1980.

———. "The Purveyor of Truth," trans. Willis Domingo et al. *Yale French Studies* 52 (1975).

Fages, Jean-Baptiste. *Comprendre Jacques Lacan*. Paris: Edouard Privat, 1971.

Felman, Shoshana. "The Originality of Jacques Lacan." *Poetics Today*, 2:1b (1980/81), 45–57.

———. "Psychoanalysis and Education: Teaching Terminable and Interminable." *Yale French Studies* 63 (1981), 21–44.

Bibliography

____. "To Open the Question." *Yale French Studies* 55–56 (1977), 5–10.

Freud, Sigmund. *Beyond the Pleasure Principle. The Standard Edition of the Complete Psychological Works of Sigmund Freud,* XVIII. London: Hogarth Press, 1953–74.

____. "The Dissolution of the Oedipus Complex." *Standard Edition,* XIX.

____. "Formulations Regarding the Two Principles in Mental Functioning." *Standard Edition,* XII.

____. *General Psychological Theory.* Ed. Philip Rieff. New York: Collier, 1963.

____. "The Infantile Genital Organization." *Standard Edition,* XIX.

____. *Inhibitions, Symptoms and Anxiety. Standard Edition,* XX.

____. "Instincts and Their Vicissitudes." *Standard Edition,* XIV.

____. *The Interpretation of Dreams.* Standard Edition, IV–V.

____. *Jokes and Their Relation to the Unconscious. Standard Edition,* VIII.

____. "Negation." *Standard Edition,* XIX.

____. *New Introductory Lectures on Psycho-analysis. Standard Edition,* XXII.

____. "Some Psychical Consequences of the Anatomical Distinction between the Sexes." *Standard Edition,* XIX.

____. *Three Essays on the Theory of Sexuality. Standard Edition,* VII.

____. *Totem and Taboo. Standard Edition,* XIII.

____. "The Uncanny." *Standard Edition,* XVII.

Gallop, Jane. *The Daughter's Seduction: Feminism and Psychoanalysis.* Ithaca: Cornell University Press, 1982. British edition: *Feminism and Psychoanalysis: The Daughter's Seduction.* London: Macmillan, 1982.

____. "Phallus/Penis: Same Difference." In *Men by Women. Women and Literature,* vol. 2 (New Series), ed. Janet Todd. New York and London: Holmes & Meier, 1981.

____. Review of *Vies et légendes de Jacques Lacan* by Catherine Clément. *SubStance* 32 (1981), 77–78.

George, François. *L'Effet 'yau de poêle: De Lacan et des lacaniens.* Paris: Hachette, 1979.

Huber, Gérard. *Conclure dit-il: sur Lacan.* Paris: Galilée, 1981.

Irigaray, Luce. *Ce sexe qui n'en est pas un.* Paris: Seuil, 1977. [*This Sex Which Is Not One,* trans. Catherine Porter with Carolyn Burke. Ithaca: Cornell University Press, 1985.]

Jacobus, Mary. "The Question of Language: Men of Maxims and *The Mill on the Floss.*" *Critical Inquiry,* 8, no. 2 (1981), 207–22.

Jakobson, Roman. *Selected Writings* II. Hague: Mouton, 1971.

Bibliography

Jameson, Fredric. "Imaginary and Symbolic in Lacan: Marxism, Psychoanalytic Criticism, and the Problem of the Subject." *Yale French Studies* 55–56 (1977), 338–95.

Johnson, Barbara. "The Frame of Reference." *Yale French Studies* 55–56 (1977), 457–505.

Kerrigan, William. "Introduction." In Smith and Kerrigan, eds., *Interpreting Lacan*.

Kremer-Marietti, Angèle. *Lacan et la rhétorique de l'inconscient*. Paris: Aubier-Montaigne, 1978.

Kristeva, Julia. "Within the Microcosm of 'The Talking Cure.'" In Smith and Kerrigan, eds., *Interpreting Lacan*.

Lacan, Jacques. "Le Désir et son interprétation," Compte-rendu par J. B. Pontalis. *Bulletin de Psychologie* 13, 5 (1959), 263–72.

———. *Ecrits*. Paris: Seuil, 1966.

———. *Ecrits*. I. Paris: Seuil, 1970.

———. *Ecrits* II. Paris: Seuil, 1971.

———. *Ecrits: A Selection*, trans. Alan Sheridan. New York: Norton, 1977.

———. *The Four Fundamental Concepts of Psychoanalysis*, trans. Alan Sheridan. New York: Norton, 1978.

———. *The Language of the Self: The Function of Language in Psychoanalysis*, trans. Anthony Wilden. Baltimore: Johns Hopkins University Press, 1968.

———. *Le Séminaire* I: *Les écrits techniques de Freud*. Paris: Seuil, 1975.

———. *Le Séminaire* II: *Le Moi dans la théorie de Freud et dans la technique de la psychanalyse*. Paris: Seuil, 1978.

———. *Le Séminaire* III: *Les psychoses*. Paris: Seuil, 1981.

———. *Le Séminaire* XI: *Les quatre concepts fondamentaux de la psychanalyse*. Paris: Seuil, 1973.

———. *Le Séminaire* XX: *Encore*. Paris, Seuil, 1975.

———. "Seminar on 'The Purloined Letter,'" trans. Jeffrey Mehlman. *Yale French Studies* 48 (1972), 38–72.

———. "Some Reflections on the Ego." *International Journal of Psychoanalysis* 34 (1953), 11–17.

Laplanche, Jean. *Vie et mort en psychanalyse*. Paris: Flammarion, 1970. [*Life and Death in Psychoanalysis*, trans. Jeffrey Mehlman. Baltimore: Johns Hopkins University Press, 1976.]

Laplanche, Jean, and Jean-Baptiste Pontalis. *Vocabulaire de la psychanalyse*. Paris: PUF, 1967. [*The Language of Psychoanalysis*, trans. Donald Nicholson-Smith. London: Hogarth, 1973.]

Bibliography

Leavy, Stanley A. "The Image and the Word: Further Reflections on Jacques Lacan." In Smith and Kerrigan, eds., *Interpreting Lacan.*

Lemaire, Anika. *Jacques Lacan.* Brussels: Pierre Mardaga, 1977. [*Jacques Lacan,* trans. D. Macey. London: Routledge & Kegan Paul, 1977.]

Lévi-Strauss, Claude. *The Elementary Structures of Kinship,* trans. James Harle Bell, John Richard von Sturmer, and Rodney Needham. Boston: Beacon Press, 1969.

Marks, Elaine. "Breaking the Bread: Gestures toward Other Structures, Other Discourses." *Bulletin of the Midwest Modern Language Association,* 13 (Spring 1980), 53–56.

Mehlman, Jeffrey. "Poe Pourri: Lacan's Purloined Letter." *Semiotexte* 1, 3 (1975), 51–68.

Miller, Jacques-Alain, ed. *L'Excommunication: La communauté psychanalytique en France II.* Paris: Bibliothèque d'Ornicar?, 1977.

———. *La Scission de 1953: La communauté psychanalytique en France I.* Paris: Bibliothèque d'Ornicar?, 1976.

Mitchell, Juliet, and Jacqueline Rose, eds. *Feminine Sexuality: Jacques Lacan and the école freudienne.* New York: Norton 1982.

Montrelay, Michèle. "Recherches sur la féminité." *Critique* 278 (1970), 654–74. ["Inquiry into Femininity," trans. Parveen Adams. *m|f* 1 (1978), 83–101.]

Muller, John P., and William J. Richardson. *Lacan and Language: A Reader's Guide to* Ecrits. New York: International Universities Press, 1982.

Nancy, Jean-Luc, and Philippe Lacoue-Labarthe. *Le Titre de la lettre.* Paris: Galilée, 1973.

Palmier, Jean-Michel. *Lacan.* Paris: Editions Universitaires, 1972.

Ragland-Sullivan, Ellie. "Jacques Lacan: Feminism and the Problem of Gender Identity." *SubStance* 36 (1982), 9–20.

Roustang, François. *Un Destin si funeste.* Paris: Minuit, 1976. [*Dire Mastery: Discipleship from Freud to Lacan.* trans. Ned Lukacher. Baltimore: Johns Hopkins University Press, 1982.]

Schneiderman, Stuart. *Jacques Lacan: The Death of an Intellectual Hero.* Cambridge: Harvard University Press, 1983.

Schneiderman, Stuart, ed. *Returning to Freud: Clinical Psychoanalysis in the School of Lacan.* New Haven: Yale University Press, 1980.

Smith, Dorothy E. "An Analysis of Ideological Structures and How Women Are Excluded." *Canadian Review of Sociology and Anthropology* 12, 4 (1975), 353–69.

Smith, Joseph H., and William Kerrigan, eds. *Interpreting Lacan.* New Haven: Yale University Press, 1983.

Stanton, Martin. *Outside the Dream: Lacan and French Styles of Psycho-analysis.* London: Routledge & Kegan Paul, 1983.

Vergote, Antoine. "From Freud's 'Other Scene' to Lacan's 'Other.' " In Smith and Kerrigan, eds., *Interpreting Lacan.*

Weber, Samuel. *The Legend of Freud.* Minneapolis: University of Minnesota Press, 1982.

Index

Index

Index

Library of Congress Cataloging in Publication Data

Gallop, Jane, 1952–
  Reading Lacan.

  Bibliography: p.
  Includes index.
  1. Lacan, Jacques, 1901–   —Addresses, essays,
lectures. 2. Psychoanalysis—Addresses, essays, lectures. I. Title.
BF173.L15G34 1985   150.19'5'0924   85–7892
ISBN 0–8014–1585–3 (alk. paper)